Fairground Architecture

Excursions into Architecture

Series editors:
John Smith
David Braithwaite

Fairground Architecture

**The World of Amusement Parks,
Carnivals, and Fairs**

by David Braithwaite

FREDERICK A. PRAEGER, *Publishers*

New York · Washington

BOOKS THAT MATTER

Published in the United States of America in 1968
by Frederick A. Praeger, Inc., Publishers
111 Fourth Avenue, New York, N.Y. 10003

Library of Congress Catalog Card Number: 68-27429

Printed in Great Britain

Contents

To the travelling showman

Introduction

In this age of complex invention, when the bounds of technology seem infinitely extended and space travel is as commonplace as the grinding to a halt through overcrowding of the road traffic in our towns and cities, the simple pleasures of the fairground may seem remote. Indeed, the very existence of such transient spectacles is to many an anachronism in this age, whilst to others it appears an ever-worsening curse. For certain inconvenience is caused to some on each occasion of a fair, which causes those concerned to act the sourpuss and killjoy, and powerful are the efforts made regularly to upset the ancient charters under which the fairs are held. Yet our social scene would be as much impoverished by the extinction of the traditional fair as by the unnecessary destruction of old buildings, for it is factors like these that provide the tangible link with the past that makes living in the present the more enjoyable. We must hope that the traditional fair, in Great Britain at least, will long continue to flourish; to continue, with its magic glitter, its noise and bustle, the clatter of the machinery of its rides and of its mechanical music, and its sham opulence, to give endless delight and pleasure to the crowds.

It is perhaps curious that the fair, unlike other traditional mobile spectacles, particularly the circus, has not been the object of greater study. For those seeking to learn about fairs and their history, the books to which they can turn are indeed few.

In the present volume, David Braithwaite, an architect who has long been an enthusiast for the subject, has collected together a wealth of information, much of which has not been published before. He has travelled the length and breadth of the country visiting fairgrounds of all types and sizes and he has here set down the results of his enquiries in the enthusiastic manner of one totally immersed in his subject. Yet although his survey has been wide and comprehensive, he would probably share the modesty of an earlier writer, Henry Morley, who prefaced his *Memoirs of Bartholomew Fair* in 1858 in part as follows:—

'Since I am here occupying virgin soil in a part of the wild district beyond the bounds of cultivated history, I may be pardoned perhaps if my ground is not at once staked out in the best manner, and my fields are not so trim as those combed by the ploughs and harrows of successive generations. This is not only the first history of Bartholomew Fair, but the first serious history of any Fair; even the general subject of Fairs, as far as I can learn, has never been thought worthy of a book. Yet what a distinct chapter in social history should be contained in the story, rightly told, of any Great National Fair! . . . .

Thus, while I may expect allowance to be made for the rough way in which I have staked out my little claim, upon virgin soil, yet is the soil so rich that I fear I must go unpardoned if it shall prove to have yielded to my tillage but a scanty harvest. Though I have raised and garnered all the knowledge I could get about the Fair, there certainly was more attainable: there are pamphlets and collections doubtless, that I have not seen; collectors whom I have not sought. I feel also that I must have overlooked, through ignorance, facts known to many of my readers. Therefore I shall be most thankful for all further information that may come to me from any source.

. . . To maids and boys I sing. The place about our standing is well swept, and there is no dirt of the Fair here to offend them.

NEVER BEFORE EXHIBITED. BARTHOLOMEW THE ROYAL SMITHFIELD GIANT. SEVEN HUNDRED YEARS OF AGE. HIS MOTHER'S AT ROME AND HIS FATHER'S AT BRADFORD. TO BE SEEN A-LIVE.'
Vivat Regina! 'Shall there be good Vapour?'
. . . 'Sith all that in the world is great and gay,
    Doth as a vapour vanish and decay—'

Ben Jonson
(Captain Knockem Jordan).

The sentiments so flamboyantly expressed by Henry Morley are in a way still relevant and the subject area remains one that can be further explored. For the showmen themselves are curiously reticent, living in a world apart, introvert and suspicious of the interest of strangers. They have suffered down the years from the bad, and most often unfair, publicity of the press. Persecuted by our legislators, perhaps unwittingly, through the Town and Country Planning Acts and the Road Licensing and Noise Abatement laws, and with a serious loss in the number of grounds available, it is small wonder that they feel somewhat outcast by society. Even winter quarters, regarded officially as caravan sites, are becoming difficult to find. Furthermore, their equipment is taxed at a high rate which makes the present purchase price of a new roundabout or dodg'em some £10,000 to £15,000, a truly major item of capital expenditure. Yet they remain an industrious and hard-working community, not a few of whom are prosperous, and who dislike intensely being confused with those other travellers, the gipsies. In spite of all these difficulties, however, it is worth noting that there are now more travelling showmen than there were in the thirties, before the last war. Clearly there is much to be said for a life on the open road.

Although a detailed study of the social structure of the fairground would not be without interest, and indeed this aspect is ever relevant, it is with the many diverse elements that form the physical environment that David Braithwaite is here concerned. He describes and comments upon the numerous sideshows and rides, with their vivid names and strange histories, and demonstrates most skilfully the development of the ingenious machines. The reader is taken round the booths and joints, as they are called, on to the exotic Razzle Dazzle, Flying Pigs, Octopus, Waltzing Balloon, the Swirl or Swish, the Wheely Whirly and Whirligig, and shown the whole layout of the fair or tober, with its variety of plans to suit individual locations, be they open fields or the narrow twisting streets in the centre of an old town.

The glossary of fairground terms, an essential and fine embellishment to the book, is rich with information. One learns that the Womp is the transitional ride between the Whip and the Swirl. That the boneshaking old Cakewalk changes its name to suit the fashion of the day, becoming at one time the Jolly Jersey Bounce and more recently the Rock an' Roll. That the vertical member of the drawbar assembly of top motion switchbacks is called a Sullivan, a name coined by a workman so it is said who, on being knocked on the head by the member in question, cried out 'Blimey, I thought it must 'ave been Sullivan!', meaning the then boxing champion, John L. Sullivan.

With its wealth of anecdotes and many fine photographs and drawings this volume reveals the splendours of the fairground scene. Here is one of the few genuine forms of folk art, the precursor to Pop, and one that remains vital even in this Batman age. Here is an architecture that is essentially mobile depending for its success in the design of ingenious components. Whilst some of our younger architects like to preach the virtues of the Plug-in City, which they see as a new concept, the fairground, a plug-in city on a small scale, has been with us for centuries. Long may it flourish. If David Braithwaite's book helps to promote interest in this neglected and much abused subject it will prove to have been a worthwhile undertaking indeed.

John Smith   South Audley Street.

Author's Note

The evanescent quality of the fair, the fabulous demountable structures, and the rich fabric of its history interwoven with splendid impresario figures and the humbler, though equally absorbing troupers, presented an irresistable challenge. My dedication to the subject was born in the 1940's, a period unique because much of the equipment then on tour dated from the 1920's and 1930's. I recall watching the late Henry Thurston's 'Autodrome' loads arriving at Northampton drawn by a steam traction engine. And in those days Nottingham Goose Fair boasted two or three 'Mont Blancs' (a ride now obsolete), three 'Moon Rockets' and the occasional frock-coated pitch-getter.

In the last ten years there has been a transformation but I am optimistic enough to believe that the changes have, for the most part, been superficial. The hierarchy of professional showmen, united in the Showmen's Guild, is stronger than ever, and their ancient craft—ever responsive to the wind of change—has a perpetual freshness. A deeply philosophical approach, an essential single-mindedness and the simple motivation of joy have a timeless quality and will, I trust, prove enduring and indestructible.

The material upon which this book was based was collected over the last seven years. I am much indebted to fellow enthusiasts, with longer memories than mine, and to the resources of their respective societies. These include Dick Taylor of the Fairground Society, Bert Barker of the British Fairground Society and Kenneth Brown of the Fairground Cine Club.

My researches in King's Lynn were particularly fruitful and my gratitude to Arthur Johnson is very considerable. His conscientious investigation at Savage's Works led to many remarkable discoveries and to the unravelling of much confused history. I am grateful, too, to Mr Stephenson Pilling, Managing Director of Savages for his generous co-operation, to Vic Walker—foreman, and to Fred Gaskin, a former employee. Miss Mottram of the King's Lynn Museum, Mr Wilson of the Library and Mr Greenfield, Editor of the *Lynn News and Advertiser*, gave much assistance.

Among many fine collections of photographs from which material has been drawn, I would mention, with appreciation, the following:—

The Fenwick Collection, Newcastle-upon-Tyne
William Keating, Wythenshawe
R. J. Woodfin, Tewkesbury

To Dennis Roberts of Cobb & Clow, who photo copied many priceless drawings as well as providing other material, and to Keith Wilson, a former school friend who very patiently took many photographs for me, I owe a special debt of gratitude.

F. C. Roope, General Secretary of the Showmen's Guild gave encouragement and provided much statistical data. Thomas Murphy kindly read and corrected the 'Glossary'. Charles Thurston was an invaluable liaison with the showmen.

I would also express my thanks to the following: Geoffrey Starmer of the Northamptonshire Industrial Archaeology Group; J. H. Bailey, Clerk of the Markets, Nottingham; Alfred Fox, Borough Treasurer, Stratford-upon-Avon; Bo Ekelund of Lasten Päivän Säätiö, Helsinki; Nikola Elphinstone of the Laing Art Gallery, Newcastle-upon-Tyne; and to fellow-writers Ronald H. Clark, Arthur Fay, Frederick Fried, and *Worlds Fair* correspondents 'Broughton' and 'Burnley Cyclist'. Closely associated with the production, secretary Frances Law, designer Lawrence Edwards, artist David Ford, proof-reader Gillian Varley and co-ordinator Colin Webb have given unfailing support, have shown much patience and have conduced this presentation. To John Smith, my co-editor, I owe a great deal—his enthusiasm and skilful guidance have been an inspiration.

Extracts from Webster's New Collegiate Dictionary, © 1961 are reproduced by permission of G. & C. Merriam Co., Publishers of the Merriam-Webster Dictionaries.

Cornelius Walford (author of *Fairs, Past and Present*) explained the absence of an historian of fairs by the following proposition:—'The fact may perhaps be accounted for in the circumstance that fairs, as now regarded, are associated with notions of frivolity?'

In sincere humility, this book attempts to document some facets of this much neglected frivolity.

David Braithwaite   London, S.W.11. December 1967.

BACKGROUND

The atmosphere of today's pleasure fair is far removed from the vigorous barter of primitive trading fairs. A 19th century chronicler of St Bartholomew's Fair in London described it as 'nondescript noise and non-conformity'. All this and the hideousness of death rites and martyrdoms constitute a curious apposition to the abandoned gaiety associated with travelling amusements. 'We're only in business for fun' reads the banner. As with the power revolution, the historical sequence has reflected many facets of social history. Unconsciously the reflection has, at times, been exaggerated—at other times stubbornly defiant of change—but the forces of advancement have brought inevitable progression.

Webster defines 'fair' in part as follows:—'A gathering of buyers and sellers at a stated time and place for trade. A festival, and sale of fancy articles, etc. ... A competitive exhibition of wares. ...' The implication is clear. The first industrial revolution—an agricultural revolution—enabled neolithic man to produce a trading surplus, the very basis of civilisation. The carriage of merchandise led to the establishing of pioneer trade routes, and this in turn to the cross-fertilisation of cultures. Thus the origin of fairs is rooted in pre-history.

In ancient Greece it is recorded that fairs were held at Olympia, Delphi, Nemea and Delos. The coincidence of these fairs with sacred feasts, with their implied truce, ensured at least a temporary neutrality, and enabled mer-

Bartholomew Fair, London, in 1728—depicted on a lady's fan

chants to move freely. Traditionally fairs held on boundaries—on neutral land —enabled rival tribes to meet for purposes of trade, and the market cross probably had its antecedent in the boundary marker. Hermes, a god of boundaries, became god of the market too, and his image was usually set up in Greek marketplaces. And in imperial Rome, booths, tents and wooden stands for shows were common. Indeed it is almost certain that the custom of holding fairs was introduced to Northern Europe by the Romans. But after the dark ages of rapine and hostilities, the sale of slaves marred their primal purpose.

But the sacred feast, so called, had other connotations. In his book *The Pagan Origin of Fairs* T. F. G. Dexter suggests that pagan festivals, associated with funeral games and worship of the dead, were held in both Stone Age and Bronze Age. On St Ann's Hill, Wiltshire, where Tan Hill Fair was held annually, the intersection of ancient trackways coincides with five round barrows. Funeral games were also a characteristic in ancient Greece, where markets were often assembled near the graves of slaughtered heroes—semi-mythical beings. Unhappily the tradition survived, and during the reign of Henry IV men and women were burnt alive as heretics, and Bartholomew Fair was then held over their ashes. Centuries later Gordon and Robertson described a fair, *c.* 1724, held near the Church of Kinnethmont, Aberdeenshire, as follows:—'. . . an old Chappel . . . and a dyke encompassing it where they are yet in the use of burying their dead. . . . There is . . . a Yearly fair called Christ's Fair and commonly the Sleepy Market, because it begins at night about sunset, and ends one hour after sunrising next morning. . . . A very singular kind of mercat, as any ever was.'

This anomaly apart, during the Roman occupation of this country many fairs were established. *Fairs, Past and Present* by C. Walford, one of the very few authoritative works on the subject, records fairs at Helston (Cornwall),

Barnwell (Cambs), Newcastle-upon-Tyne, and several places along the line of the Roman wall in Northumberland. These were re-instituted in the 9th century, and the number was probably added to by the Saxons. The Normans introduced Church Feasts in order that trade might attract those whom religion could not influence, and indeed a substantial part of the Monasteries' income came through the sale of 'home produce'. Thereafter identity of origin becomes obscure.

After the collapse of the Roman Empire and the gradual decline of the feudal system the emergent social structure gave incentive to the craftsmen. A parallel revolution in agriculture, based on an essentially modern form of plough and the hinged flail for threshing, led to unprecedented commercial expansion throughout Europe. Large trading fairs were established, and under the terms of Magna Carta (1215) 'All merchants shall have safety and security in coming into England and going out of England, and in staying and in travelling through England, as well by land as by water, to buy and sell without any unjust exactions according to ancient and right customs. . . .' The most important of these fairs was held at Stourbridge.* Assembled in a field near Barnwell monastery, in September of each year, there were booths for the sale of pottery, oysters (from the port of Lynn), clothing, iron goods, hats, gloves, hops, wool, waggon cloth, silks and toys. There were separate markets for the sale of horses, cheese, baskets and onions. The rivers Ouse and Cam were vital transport arteries.

Walford records that in France, too, fairs were established at Champagne and Brie where merchants from Italy and Spain congregated. The Genoese sent bales of silks, Burgundy sent cloth, Catalonia leather. In Flanders, the weekly markets at Bruges, Courtray, Torhout and Monteasel primarily dealt in woollen goods. By the close of the 16th century, Antwerp had two six-week fairs where bills of exchange valid in all parts of Europe were used.

Thus from the church graveyard full of traders, pedlars loitering in the porches and, in the words of Bishop Richard Poore of Salisbury writing in the 15th century, ' dances or vile and indecorous games which tempt to unseemliness ', a miraculous transformation was taking place. And in this transformation unfolded many aspects of popular entertainment that ultimately were to be the principal attractions of the fair. An historical survey, based on Henry Morley's *Memoirs of Bartholomew Fair*, illustrates the point. Established in 1120 by a grant from Henry I to a monk who had formerly been his jester, Bartholomew Fair was first held in the priory churchyard. A feat of skill, performed for money, is recorded in ancient carved work—here a woman is depicted balancing herself head downwards, by the palms of the hands, on two sword points—all to the accompaniment of tabor and pipes. Religious miracles

* Formerly Sterebrigg. c. 1211 King John granted a charter to the lepers of the hospital of St. Mary Magdalene. A new charter was granted in 1553. From Our Old English Fairs *by R. W. Muncey.*

between 1144 and 1174 ensured a church full of worshippers, and the pleasure fair gradually receded from graveyard to market place.

In 1305 men and women were sold, and in 1400, during the days of special persecution, there were tournaments and martyrdoms. In 1539 the fair was severed from the Church, and in the following 100 years it was suspended four times by plague, in 1593, 1603, 1625 and 1630.

Although the earliest dramas were performed around 1500 there is little documentation on the subject. The first ' Wild Beast ' shows appeared in the late 1660's but 10 years later came the first attempt at suppression.

Trading went into sharp decline, and in 1691 the duration of the fair was reduced to three days. This curtailment was not, however, effective, and in subsequent years there were three further attempts at ' punctual limitation ', in 1694, 1711 and 1719. A contemporary journalist described the fair as follows:—'...a mere Carnival, a season of the utmost Disorder and Debauchery, by reason of the Booths for Drinking, Music, Dancing, Stage-plays, Drolls (presumably jesters), Lotteries, Gaming, Raffling and what not.' But the vitality of ' Bart's Fair ' was very considerable. In 1762 George Alexander Stevens described it as follows:—

' Here's Punch's whole play of the gun-powder plot, Sir,
With beasts all alive, and pease-porridge all hot, Sir;
Fine sausages fry'd, and the black on the wire,
The whole court of France, and nice pig at the fire,
Here's the ups and downs; who'll take a seat in the chair-o?
Tho' there's more up and downs than at Bartlemew fair-o.

Here's Whittington's cat, and the tall dromedary,
The chaise without horses, and queen of Hungary:
Here's the merry-go-rounds, come who rides ... Sir?
Wine, beer, ale, and cakes, fire-eating besides, Sir:
The fam'd learn'd dog that can tell all his letters,
And some men, as scholars, are not much his betters.'

The theatrical booths of Richardson, Saunders, Henry Fielding and Penkethman were well known in the first half of the 18th century, although in 1697 and again in 1700 plays and puppet shows had been prohibited. Pidcock's Wild Beast Show* was able to increase admission charges to one shilling per person —a great deal in those days—and by the turn of the century Bart's Fair had become very profitable for the showmen. The following meticulous details of cash returns for 1827 are recorded by Walford:—

* *According to E. H. Bostock* (Menageries, Circuses and Theatres) *the earliest record of a Menagerie is that of Pidcock's in 1708. Polito's show was thriving in 1805, but 30 years later a disaster while crossing the Irish Channel resulted in total loss.*

Wombwell's Menagerie . .	£1,700
Richardson's Theatre . . .	£1,200
Atkins' Menagerie	£1,000
Morgan's Menagerie	£150
Pig-faced Lady	£150
Fat Boy and Fat Girl	£150
Head of Maria Marten's Murderer (Wm. Corder) .	£100
Ballard's Menagerie	£90
Ball's Theatre	£80
Diorama of Battle of Navarino .	£60
Chinese Jugglers	£50
Pike's Theatre	£40
A Fire-Eater	£30
Frazer's Theatre	£26
Keyes & Line's Theatre	£20
'Scotch' Giant	£20

In 1839 further measures were taken to suppress the fair; eleven years later the last proclamation was made by a Lord Mayor. The London City Mission pointed out the dangers of moral pollution, the markets committee increased tolls, and by 1855 Bart's Fair was dead.

The history of Stourbridge Fair is in many ways similar. In 1604 a royal mandate prohibited ' all manner of unprofitable or idle games plays or exercise . . . especially bull-baiting, bear-baiting, common plays, publick shews, interludes, comedies and tragedies in the English tongue, games at loggets, nine holes, and all other sports and games whereby throngs, concourse or multitudes are drawn together.'

In 1748, Hussey's Great Theatrical Booth presented ' Harlequin's Frolics ' or ' Jack Spaniard caught in a Trap ', and Hone's *Year Book* of 1827 describes shows of wild beasts and wild men, conjurors, tumblers and rope dancers, Mr. Baker's company of *comedians*, Lewy Owen the clown 'full of eccentric wit and grimmace ' and other shows occupied by giants and dwarfs, whilst extending ' with stunning din along this noisy line ' were fruit and ginger bread stalls. Yet in 1855 Cambridge University called the fair for the last time; thereafter trade declined, and in 1882 only the horse fair, onion fair, and sales of wooden implements remained. The last Stourbridge Fair was held in 1927.

Fairs held primarily for the hiring of domestic and agricultural labour were known as ' Statute ' or ' Mop ' Fairs. F. C. Roope, in his book *Come to the Fair*, suggests that *statute* derives either from the Statute of Labourers of 1349, or from the Latin verb ' to stand ' implying a parade of workers for employment. *Mop* on the other hand, according to at least one other authority, is reputed to be a distortion of the Roman *mappa*, a title given to public games and originated by Nero's signal for the games to commence. The Emperor ordered the *mappa* or napkin with which he wiped his fingers after eating to be thrown out of the window. The more obvious association with ' Mrs. Mop ' is too convenient an explanation.

Among the fairs held on special historic occasions, the Thames Frost Fair was unique. The river bed was then much wider and ice that formed at both sides sometimes extended from bank to bank. Frost Fairs were held in 1564, 1608, 1684 (five weeks' duration), 1739-1740, 1788-1789, and in 1814. On this last occasion the river froze after seven days of fog. There were streets of booths, meat roasting—even a printing press, and coaches plied from Westminster to the Temple. With puppet plays, sleds and sliding with skates, interludes, cooks tipping and other lewd practices, it earned from John Evelyn the epithet ' a bacchanalian triumph, or carnival on water '.

The 19th century witnessed new prime movers—first steam, then elec-

A contemporary engraving of the 1814
Thames Frost Fair—there is a peep show
in the right foreground

The Mop Fair at Stratford-upon-Avon in 1907. Built up in the main streets of the town, the market cross—behind Bennett's 'Racing Cars'—insignificant against the 'Helter Skelters'

tricity, a new form of transportation in the railway, and the achievement of instantaneous communication, all these with far-reaching implications. Machines were very successful indeed, and there seemed no limit to the rate of progress. For the first time consumer goods were produced in such profusion as to be universally available. But mass production involved systematic distribution, warehousing, and ultimately the department store. The trading fair began to lose its importance.

Travelling showmen, sensitive to the wind of change, their tissues hardened by centuries of grafting, captured the instant with consummate skill, translating the dreams and aspirations of the new working class into tangible forms of amusement and delight. New miracles of the industrial revolution gave to the fairground an unprecedented exuberance. The *joy ride*, vivid colours, brilliant lights and instant music became all-pervading. Whereas the mediæval mind—fearful, often full of remorse and brooding—was purged by the huge actions of players in the theatre booths, a more wholesome extrovert quality now emerged.

Because of the successful transition from trading to pleasure many of the great fairs have survived. Curiosity, competition and movement are still the essence of the showman's art. Spectacular tournaments and exhibitions of inhuman cruelty have substantially disappeared, but the circus and freak show remain. The peep show finally graduated to the ' Bioscope Show ', and games of skill and chance remain part of the essential fabric. With the harnessing of steam, and later of electricity, the roundabout assumed a new importance, became the pivot of the fairground and an art form in its own right.

In 1889 the United Kingdom Van-Dwellers' Protection Association was formed to safeguard the business of the travelling showman. The organised vigorous defence of traveller's rights successfully countered George Smith's proposed Moveable Dwellings Bill for Sanitation and Education of Van Dwellers, and the Inspector of Nuisances implied by this legislation. ' Sit down, and go 'ome, Smith, we don't want you, nor none of your 'ations ', observed one showman, quoted by Rev. J. Howard Swinstead in his book *A Parish on Wheels.*

Later known as the Showmen's Guild, the association was registered in 1918 as a Trade Union. A code of rules then drawn up duly strengthened the Guild. *The Times* in 1957 reported as follows:—' As a professional body and Employers' Trade Union the Showmen of Britain must rank as one of the best governed and most co-operative in the kingdom '.

In Great Britain an average of 200 fairs are held each week during the season. Many of these are administered by local authorities through Markets and Fairs Departments, some by individual showmen, others by regional sections of the Showmen's Guild, of which there are ten:—London and Home Counties; Midland; Norwich and Eastern Counties; Derbyshire, Nottinghamshire, Mid and South Lincolnshire; Lancashire; Yorkshire; Northern; Scottish; Western; and South Wales.

Movement still exhilarates, powered revolution still inspires mechanised jubilation. The ' Waltzer ' is now a very popular ride, there are still a handful of ' Cakewalks ', and the ' Twist ', a brand new machine, has made its inevitable debut. The transport revolution has been reflected in a succession of devices from the ' Channel Tunnel Railway ', ' Motor-Car Scenics ', ' Dodg'em Cars ' and ' Flying Chair-o-Planes ' to present day ' Space-Cruisers ' and ' Hurricane Jets '.

Fairs today are less uninhibited, brasher, much less ornate, but they provide an essential outlet. Part of a fine tradition giving pleasure to thousands, they are free as the wind, vital, and seemingly indestructible.

THE TOBER

When open space becomes fairground, a miracle is wrought—and a *tober* created. The transmuting of crocodile-like road trains into this charged and exhilarating atmosphere is the phenomenon of a culture apart. The travelling showman works out his nomadic existence with the compounded skill of past ages, and with a floridity inherited perhaps from the merchants of pre-history. His total immersion in 'the business', the qualities of resolution and impenetrability, merely intensify the mystique of his art. A sensitivity to the ups and downs of life, to the fluctuation in good spirits, is almost the only point of contact with the outside world. Indeed there is an acute susceptibility to these influences—the inevitable pollination and cross-fertilisation of a community constantly on the move. Thus the *tober*, as presented, is an outward manifestation, the medium for expressions of joy and excitement, of insatiable curiosity, and less often of remorse and grief. After the Napoleonic wars, peep shows recorded in gory detail the triumphs of Wellington and Nelson; in the early 1900's there were 'Bioscope Shows', and the internal combustion engine was celebrated in the 'Motor-Car Switchback'. Today there are 'Flying Jets' and the 'Satellite'.

The fabric of the *tober* is self-transcending, insubstantial, but powerful in impact. Fantasy and sham opulence often contrast strikingly with the eroded waste ground that forms the *gaff*. But insubstantial though it may be, the

Fairground Architecture

whirling frames ablaze with lights—the innumerable excursions into delight—create a metamorphosis in terms of environment. The existing town pattern is forgotten and dreary surroundings are thrown into shadow as the dream intensifies.

The *tober* is a composite of many elements—roundabouts, booths, *joints*, and transport vehicles. There are not many rules for establishing their inter-relationship but in broad terms it is the function of side shows to define and enclose the ground. Lorries and living vans at the perimeter act somewhat as fortifications—like a city wall, and tractors interspersed among the *rides* are employed as service units supplying light and power. But in architectural terms the roundabout is the pivot. As the climax of movement, light and sound, it is the generator of the total environment, as well as being a setting-out point for the planners. Mechanical evolution has produced a structural form

Hyde Park Fair on the day of Queen Victoria's coronation—a grid-iron pattern with roundabouts at each of the four corners. Richardson's Theatrical Booth is sited prominently at the end of the central avenue

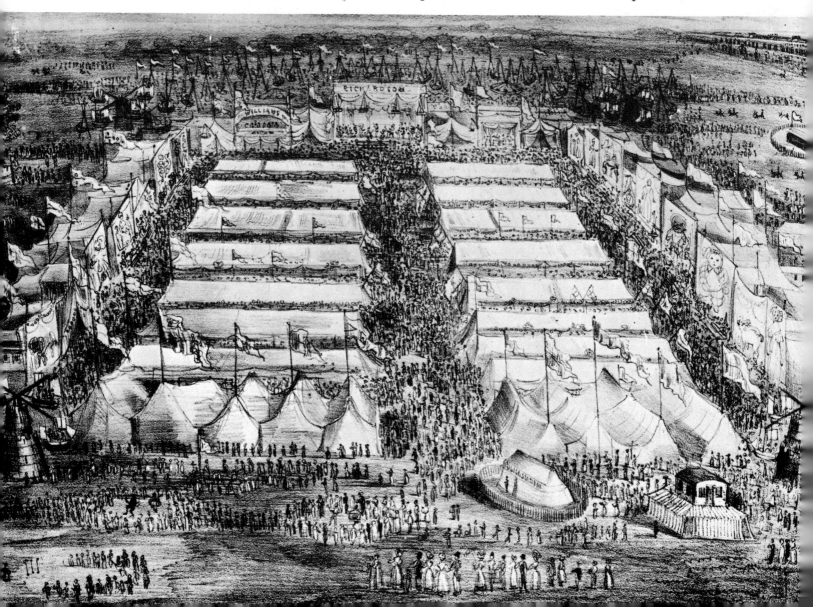

that *side and middle stuff* merely surrounds.

But it has not always been so. In 1723, when Defoe visited Stourbridge Fair, he described it, in part, as follows:—' The shops are placed in rows like streets, whereof one is call'd Cheapside . . . from London came Goldsmiths, Toyshops, Braziers, Turners, Milliners, Haberdashers, Hatters, Mercers, Drapers, Pewterers, China Warehouses, Taverns, Brandy Shops and Eating Houses. A formal great Square, form'd by the largest booths, built in that form, and which they call'd the Duddery (the old word Dudde signified cloth) —a most orderly place—80-100 yards square.'

The implied grid-iron pattern, an obvious plan form for the larger trading fairs, persisted for many years. With booths constructed as two rooms—a shop in front and living quarters behind—it was an ideal arrangement.

More than a century later the fair held in Hyde Park to celebrate the corona-

An aerial view of Hull Fair with more than 40 *rides*, 100 round stalls and some 5,500 ft. of *side stuff*. There is a full scale circus among the shows

tion of Queen Victoria followed precedent. There was, however, an interesting departure—roundabouts were placed at each of the four corners.

When the emphasis finally switched from trade to pleasure the relationship between booth and roundabout was completely reversed. Indeed the core of the *tober* became like a gigantic mechanism with the larger circles of roundabouts meshing with a complex of smaller round stalls, the space between essentially fluid and perhaps deliberately confusing. In all but the great pleasure fairs—like Newcastle, Hull and Nottingham—axial planning, with wide avenues of approach, seems destined to failure. There is, perhaps, a rule of inversion between density of crowd and the rate of spending *pro rata*.

Booths and *joints* jostling for space, like Delphic treasuries on the sacred way, now reflect the roundabout idiom and attempt competition in terms of light and colour. But they are usually more successful in their persuasive intimacy. More than enclosure, they create a vortex about the *rides*, and afterwards despatch the *punters* hither and thither on seductive spending routes.

Using the elements of *joint* and *round'un*, entrance systems are normally contrived to act as funnels. Vistas in the grand manner are rarely possible, but often there are views of fine—if accidental—graphic quality. The suggestion of deeper roundings—the sudden glimpse of a roundabout in motion—are all-important. Vertical features like the 'Big Wheel', 'Helter Skelter' and 'Chair-o-Planes', with their geometric patterns of electric lamps, are valuable advertising symbols—sometimes they are augmented by the beams from searchlights. A good showman will never neglect this visual emphasis, particularly when the ground can be seen from some distance.

The composite plan of Nottingham Goose Fair held in October on the Forest Site is a case in point. The north and south corner entrances are obvious funnels, the central entry on Gregory Boulevard is a contrived piece of axial

Anderton and Rowland's Fair at St. Blazey, Cornwall, in September, 1925— the larger circles of roundabouts meshing with a complex of smaller round stalls

An entrance funnel to Nottingham Goose Fair

GREGORY BOULEVARD

NOEL STREET

NORTH

Plan of the 1965 Nottingham Goose Fair   *(key overleaf)*

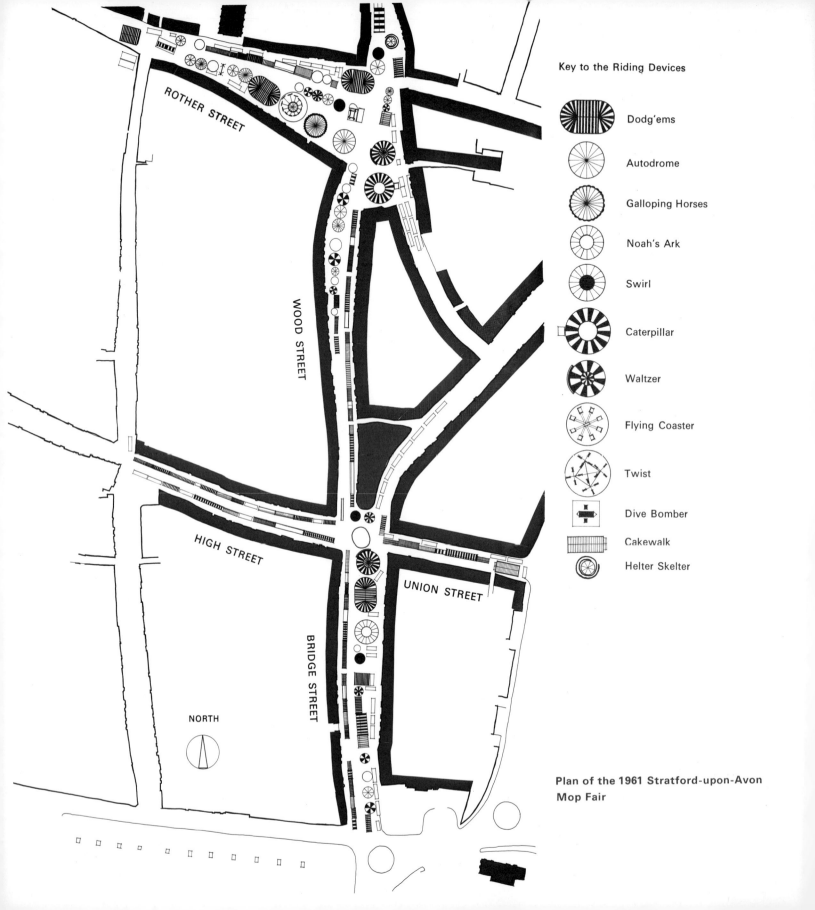

Key to the Riding Devices

Dodg'ems

Autodrome

Galloping Horses

Noah's Ark

Swirl

Caterpillar

Waltzer

Flying Coaster

Twist

Dive Bomber

Cakewalk

Helter Skelter

ROTHER STREET

WOOD STREET

HIGH STREET

BRIDGE STREET

UNION STREET

NORTH

Plan of the 1961 Stratford-upon-Avon
Mop Fair

Octopus

 Flying Saucers

 Calypso

 Hurricane Jets

Tipping Vampire Jets

Satellite

 Paratrooper

 Moon Rocket

 Steam Yachts

 Twin Big Wheels

 Juvenile

planning, whereas the north-west entry has fine accidental vistas. The western approach from Noel Street is like a roller conveyor. There are tight clusters of *round'uns* confining some of the larger riding machines, two central arcades—intimate in scale, and the occasional wide avenue. Shows are concentrated in the south-west corner, their *walk-up* fronts forming an 'L'. 'Helter Skelters', twin 'Big Wheels' and the 'Steam Yachts' are carefully placed to give vertical emphasis.

As with many of the larger fairs, the layout of Goose Fair is initiated by the City Markets and Fairs Department, who have their own practical considerations to reconcile. Space must be left for withdrawing the emptied packing trucks, and for the entry of service vehicles, ambulances and fire-engines. On the other hand, the question of maximum revenue for the three-day fair does not go unnoticed. Revenue comes, quite simply, from the rentals paid by showmen—a lump sum for *machine* positions, and a unit price per foot run of side-show. This latter consideration is perhaps even more pronounced at Hull Fair which has a higher density.

The rigid containment of Market Square and High Street imposes more severe planning disciplines on the ancient Charter Fairs. With traffic diverted, shopping precincts invaded and display windows blinded by the backs of *joints*, the town pattern and its commercial functioning becomes—for a day or two—quite obsolete. But the superimposed *pleasure grid* adds, as it were, a dimension of pique. Imagine the surprise of finding in Union Street (Stratford-upon-Avon) a 'Cakewalk' and a 'Haunted Castle', in Wood Street a 'Double-Headed Cuban Giant', and in Rother Street no less than eight large roundabouts. Building up and pulling down has to be done in the night hours and the clearance of showmen's vehicles involves very precise timing. Street fairs are mostly confined to one day, and Mop Fairs are concentrated in the autumn—a season described by showmen as the 'back end run'.

The village green, the Heath and Stray are quite a different story. Here the *tober* can be assembled around natural features and be complementary to them. The shade offered by large trees can be used to advantage, and the interpenetration of external space is the best possible funnel. With plenty of ground available, and the detail layout invariably left to the showman-lessee, there is every opportunity for an ideal solution. Blind spots and bad *machine* positions (there are some at Nottingham) should not occur. The peripheral ring of *side stuff* can be broken when rental is not critical thus permitting entry from all sides. The ultimate development lies in the open-sided fair with the core of the *tober* open to a road, a footpath or a riverbank.

Differing site conditions add spontaneity to the layout. The manner in which the elements are collected and set out is part of the *super* showman's

Fairground Architecture

An aerial view of Potters Bar Fair—
typical of country fairs

Holiday makers picnic in the shade at
London's Hampstead Heath Fair—
August, 1935

artistry. It is largely intuitive and much influenced by the visual impact—by day and by night. There is little definable logic about the induced flow of *punters*, and knowledge of the constructional limitations—space to build up and to off-load from vehicles—is simply born of experience. It cannot be taught.

There are three identifiable categories of building in the *tober*, three distinct and essential components: the *rides*—roundabouts, 'Dodg'ems' and the like, booths and *joints* that are called *side and middle stuff*, and transport vehicles, which include showmen's living vans. Of course there are sub-categories, and sometimes the divisions are not so distinct. For example, a vehicle can be constructed as a booth, occasionally a *ride* is built into or around a road truck, and some shows—the 'Ghost Train' is one—incorporate a *ride*. 'Swing Boats' and 'Helter Skelter' are, in a sense, accessories to the roundabout, and *tober furniture*—the *striker*, coin-freed machines, balloon, candy floss and novelty vendors—are essentially *side and middle* adjuvants.

The transport revolution, finding inevitable reflection in contemporary roundabout cars, also transformed showmen's road trains. A hundred years ago the horse predominated, and trucks—even roundabout parts—were specially designed for coupling to the shafts. In the era of the steam road locomotive, loads increased both in weight and size. The less temperamental petrol lorry, and later the diesel tractor, permitted the development of articulated vehicles on which *rides* and shows could literally be folded up.

The three categories are explored in some detail in the following pages. The origin and development of specific components are outlined against the background of history. Twentieth century trends are discussed and a newly-emerged vitality assessed in Chapter six.

Nottingham Goose Fair—the *tober* nears completion

THE JOY RIDE

Axles and wheels emerged out of the neolithic fog around 3,500 BC, allegedly a Sumerian invention. Man was then a tiller of the ground, struggling to achieve an agricultural surplus. Tools were primitive, and human muscles—later those of the ox—were the only reliable prime movers. The discovery of the use of wind to drive sailing ships coincided roughly with the invention of the wheel, but clearly the inorganic force of wind was both intermittent and changeable.

As a fundamental invention the wheel enjoyed only limited success. Indeed some 2,000 years passed before the spoked wheel came into common usage. Diameters then increased, pulleys and geared mechanisms were evolved, and about 450 BC the Greeks pioneered the crane. But without a powerful driving force the actual possibilities could not be fully realised. The domination of the ruling classes in early civilisations, coupled with the comparative scarcity of bronze tools, tended, in any case, to inhibit inventiveness.

Iron tools were widely used in Palestine, Syria, Asia Minor and Greece from about 1,000 BC, but the subsequent diversion of human energy to warfare, the rise and fall of Greek and Roman empires, may have had the effect of retarding technical progress. Notwithstanding this the widespread use of iron tools led to the emergence of a new social structure. The production of a greater agricultural surplus enabled an increased number of specialised crafts-men, freed from necessity to till the ground, to work out fully the possibilities of this new metal.

The water wheel, invented about 100 BC, energised the expanding Mediæval society. According to the Domesday Book there were more than 5,000 in England, and by the middle of the 15th century water wheels were used for forge hammers and bellows, saw mills, mine pumping and winding, and iron rolling mills. They yielded an efficiency equal to that of 100 slaves, as did the windmill, a later invention. But both could do so only in favourable geomorphic and climatic conditions. Man was still the most reliable and adaptable prime mover.

Thus the wheel grew to terrifying proportions and achieved a peak of domination. Agricola describes sturdy water wheels more than forty feet in height, but he also describes a wheel in which men were imprisoned—a tread-mill in fact. With all available sources of energy severely taxed, enslavement to the wheel was inevitable.

Mechanical inventiveness had solved many problems, machines were seen to be essentially successful, ideas abundant and communicated through the printing press, but a new prime mover was urgently needed. The spirit of the period was epitomised in the note-books of Leonardo da Vinci—5,000 pages of meticulously-recorded mechanical inventions ranging from trip hammer to flying machine—some practicable, others fundamentally unsound. But an overall lack of technical experience prevented their fulfilment, as would the lack of power their useful application.

Subsequent industrialisation made heavy demands on coal-mining resulting in the sinking of deeper shafts, and this in turn presented the acute problem of providing adequate pumping machinery. The horse whim and rag-and-chain pump, balls of horsehair packed into a vertical tube—could no longer cope. Yet it was this primitive mechanism, and this acute need, that ultimately led to the harnessing of steam power. In 1712 Newcomen constructed his first engine with separate piston and cylinder, using the cycle expansion—condensation—vacuum, more or less the reverse of the cycle of the suction pump. But the vertical pump stroke of his engines could not actuate the wheel.

It was left to James Watt to develop the reciprocating steam engine, and this he patented in 1781. More than 70,000 horse power of steam was being used in cotton mills alone by 1850, and the Watt engine was soon in general use for printing, threshing, flour milling, coal and copper mining.

Despite the evils of the emergent factory system—low wages, long hours, child·labour and foul conditions—the standard of living continued to rise, and eventually the workers were able to share in the abundance of commodities they produced. Thus the steam engine revolutionised industry and transportation too, freed man from the whim and relegated the treadmill to a form of corrective punishment.

VIEW OF THE TREAD MILL FOR THE EMPLOYMENT OF PRISONERS,
ERECTED AT THE HOUSE OF CORRECTION AT BRIXTON BY MR WM CUBITT OF IPSWICH.
RECOMMENDED BY THE COMMITTEE OF THE SOCIETY
FOR THE IMPROVEMENT OF PRISON DISCIPLINE &c.

The treadmill relegated to a form of
corrective punishment

Throughout time, the aim of man, beyond survival, has been to produce a surplus. Surplus led to trade, and trade to the establishing of markets and fairs. Trade routes and travelling merchantmen, like the Midianites described in Genesis, are implicit in this development. But surplus also led to joy, and to the expression of joy through music, and also through movement. The harnessing of adequate prime movers at once released man from the toil of wheel-spinning and made possible wheel-riding—joy-riding.

The resolution of technological problems which formerly hindered man's advancement was cause enough for both joy and exuberance, and the urge to express this was instrumental in transforming the basic gyrations and oscillations of productive machinery into contrivances for amusement. With the conquest of reciprocating motion the ever-increasing multiplicity of wheels were turned on their backs, as it were, to provide pleasurable movement. The tread-mill achieved its counterpart in the ' Big Wheel ', the steam roundabout and switchback; the steam swing and ' Razzle Dazzle ' drew inspiration from mechanisms in the spinning frame, the power loom, forge hammer and threshing machine.

Although it is not clear when the concept of joy-riding emerged, one thing is established—that all roundabouts are based on the spoked wheel. Peter Mundy, who visited the Feast of Biram at Phillippopolis *c.*1620, describes one thus:—' . . . like a great cart wheel, on whose circumference are fastened little seats, wherein the children being sat the wheel is put about, they all going round horizontal wise '.

Much earlier, a Byzantine bas-relief, *c.* 500, noted by Frederick Fried in his book *A Pictorial History of the Carousel*, depicts acrobats, jugglers, bears, and spectators watching two riders suspended in baskets from a centre pole.

The word *carousel* derives from an equestrian sport practised in Arabia and Turkey during the 12th century. Clay balls filled with scented water were thrown from one horseman to another—the object being to make a safe catch. Some 300 years later, transformed into an elaborate spectacle and performed by troops of cavalrymen, the *carousel* became popular in France and Germany, an important feature being the ring spearing tournament. The Moorish origin of this contest, together with the strange blending of history and mythology, inspired rich and utterly fantastic decorations, elements of which were crystallised in early manufactured roundabouts. The provision for spectators on the sidelines is a vital part of amusement devices today.

In a letter to the Patent Office dated 1673 Raphaell Folyarte describes an invention known as the ' Royalle Carousell ':—' A new and rare invencon knowne by the name of the royalle carousell or tournament, being framed and

Three several sorts of Swingings—
roundabout, wheel and swing: an
illustration from *The Travels of Peter
Mundy in Europe and Asia, 1608-1667*

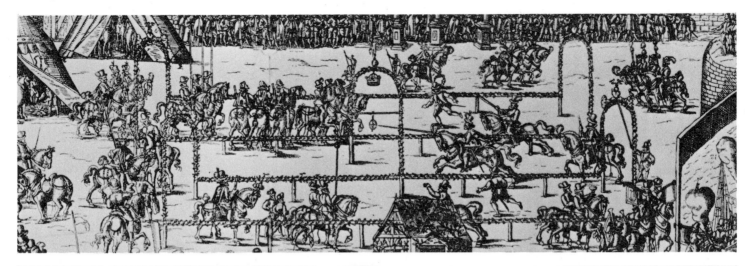

A ring spearing contest at the Court of Brandenburg, 1592

Mr. J. takes a ride at St. Cloud.
A roundabout with an extended centre pole, and tie rods to the spoke ends: notice the manual propulsion of both this and the 'Wheel' in the background

contrived with such engines as will not only afford great pleasure to us and our nobility in the sight thereof, but sufficient instruction to all such ingenious young gentlemen as desire to learne the arte of perfect horsemanshipp with all the usual practices and exercises thereof. . . .' Thus the *carousel* became mechanised.

With the spoked wheel as common denominator, advancing designs had the axle, or centre pole, longer, and the wheel suspended from it. Tension rods from the top of the centre pole to the spoke ends later served as rafters for the canvas *tilt*. Platforms slung between spokes carried crude legless horses—sometimes carriages. The cruciform hub, formed of two baulks of timber, made the whole machine transportable.

In his book *Seventy Years a Showman* Lord George Sanger describes a roundabout built by his father c. 1865: ' My father had manufactured a very primitive kind of roundabout. The horses were enlarged examples of the rough penny toys. Their legs were simply stiff round sticks; their bodies were lumps of deal rounded on one side; their heads were roughly cut from half-inch deal boards and inserted in a groove in the bodies, while the tails and manes were made of strips of rabbit skin. They were gaudy animals, however, their coats of paint being white, plentifully dotted with red and blue spots. Motive power was obtained from the boys at the fairs, who, having no half-pennies of their own, were always ready to push round their luckier companions for the reward of a ride later on.'

Within the limits of available motive power—first boys at the fair as described by Sanger, then ponies harnessed to the inside of a carriage—the spoked wheel increased in diameter, the number of spokes being multiplied so that eight pairs of horses and two carriages could be suspended. Carriages seating six adults, with carved panels and painted in bright colours, are described by Thomas Murphy in his paper *The Evolution of Amusement Machines*. But beyond this point development was only possible when the steam engine was harnessed.

In 1863 DeAth set down proposals for steam machinery to actuate ' flying and swinging boats ', ' see-saws ' and ' merry-go-rounds '. Two years later, at Aylsham Fair, Norfolk, Sidney George Soame presented the first steam-driven roundabout—at least it was the first one on record. Utilising flat belt drive, the machine could not have been wholly satisfactory, due to the friction on starting up with a full load. Frederick Savage, an agricultural engineer who lived in a neighbouring parish to Soame, saw the machine and decided to develop the idea at his works in King's Lynn.

Many original drawings and documents have survived, but it is not clear whether Savage's first steam-driven roundabout was a ' set of horses ' or a

A manually-propelled 'Velocipede'
roundabout built by Frederick Savage
and reputed to be as early as 1861

'Velocipede'—one or two rows of velocipedes (early bicycles) arranged about a circular grooved track. A family biography suggests the latter, and claims this to be Savage's own un-patented invention. Fried suggests otherwise, describing an American invention called the 'Velocipede Carrousel' that appeared in France in 1869. The *Lynn News* records the annual Mart of 1866 as follows:—'The annual fair was being held at Lynn. . . . In addition to the bazaars, gingerbread and try stalls, there are Mr. Douglas's theatre, Mr. Clayton's interesting mechanical exhibition, Case's marionettes, Mr. Ambrose's gallery of art, rifle galleries, shows, roundabouts (one steam one) etc. etc.'

The roundabout referred to was probably a 'Velocipede', similar to the one illustrated on the Savage letterhead. In 1870 Savage built 'Velocipede' machines, all steam-driven, for showmen Hough (February), Charles Bugg (June) and Pettigrove (October).

Frederick Savage & Co. Limited letter head, c. 1895

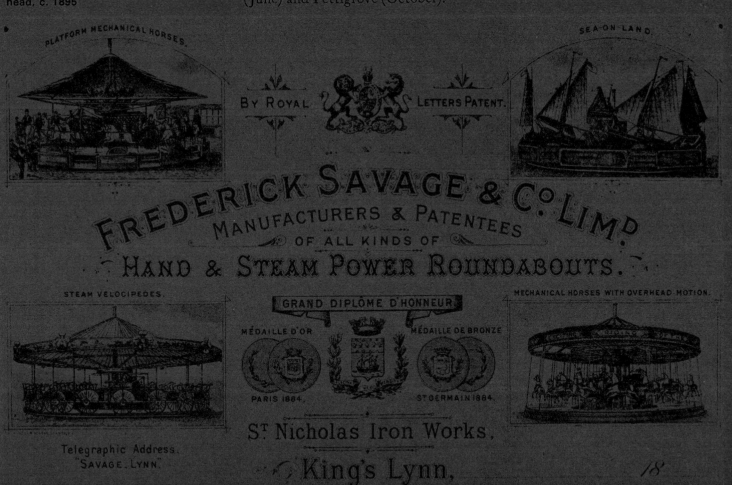

39

But more important was the evolution of the *centre truck* which was, and still is, the essential component of the travelling roundabout. Frederick Savage must be wholly credited with this—he designed and built a roundabout centre engine mounted on a stout sprung truck complete with trams and overhead gear-work. The drive, by crown wheel and pinion, engaged with the centre hub or *cheese* wheel, from which the spokes radiated. The spokes became known as *swifts*, the engine truck as *centre truck*, and the whole rotating frame (the spoked wheel), from which carriages and horses were suspended, the *spinning frame*. With brightly polished brass fittings, best gunmetal gauges and cocks, steam harmony whistles or sirens, Savage centre engines were fine pieces of work, and have now become collectors' items.

The *centre truck* represented a complete statement of the harnessing of steam—to joy-riding it was as significant as was Watt's rotative patent to

Centre truck on trams with engine mounted longitudinally, as illustrated in Savage's 1902 Catalogue

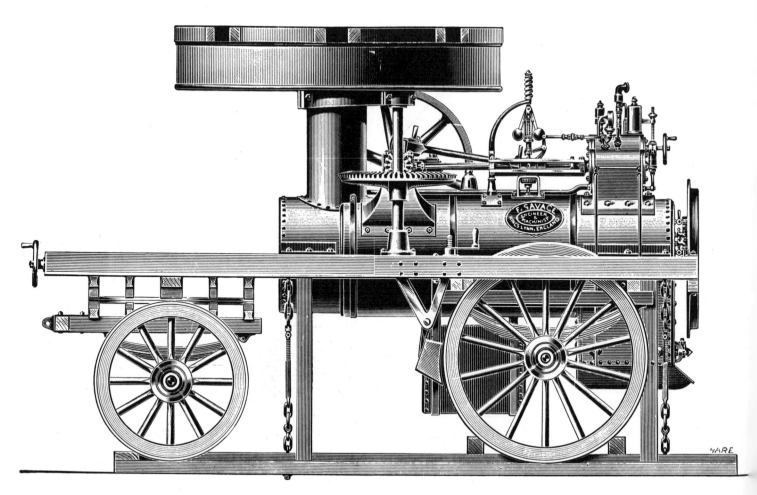

(above) The Savage '5½' *centre engine* designed for transverse mounting and standard for most of the 'Gallopers'

(right) George Twigdon & Sons' 'Sea-on-Land' roundabout photographed in the 1890s

(below) Fred Hodder's 'Chinese Junks' c. 1890—a large top *tilt* with *rounding boards* took the place of sails and awnings

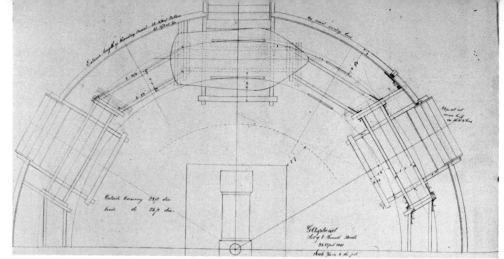

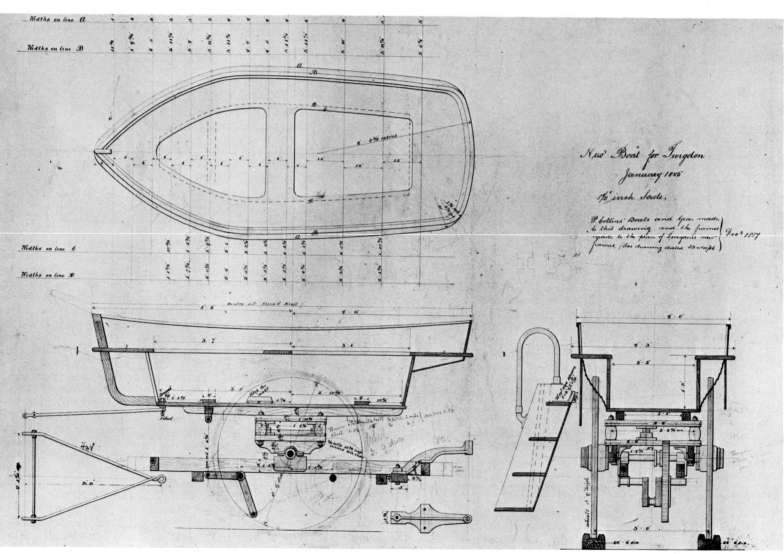

New Boat for Twigdon
January 1855

1½ inch Scale.

industry. Larger roundabouts could now be built, a faster ride achieved, and later complex mechanisms, compounding vertical and horizontal motion, could be introduced.

In partnership with William Sanger of Margate, Savage patented the ' Sea-on-Land ' roundabout in 1880. Consisting of six *yachts* propelled about a circular track, the ride incorporated a rolling and pitching motion, described by the makers as resembling ' the rocking of a boat at sea. . . .' Showman George Twigdon took delivery of one of the first sets in April-May 1881. A lighthouse concealing the smoke stack is a typical elaborately-detailed foible. There was a more sophisticated set, known as Fred Hodder's ' Chinese Junks ', but subsequent dispute between the partners arising out of the apportionment of royalties led·to the abandonment of this venture. The rolling and pitching motion was adapted to the ' Gondola Switchback ', which is described later.

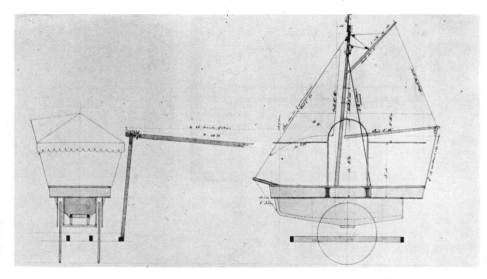

(opposite page top) Original drawing of George Aspland's 'Sea-on-Land' round-about, 1881. George Aspland, a grocer from Holbeach, started his career on the fairground as a photographer. This proved so profitable that he quickly became a roundabout proprietor, and so successful was this *machine* that a terrace of houses in Boston, Lincolnshire, was purchased with the profits. They still exist and bear the name 'Sea-on-Land Terrace'

A detail of the new *boat* built for Twigdon in 1885. The cross-section shows the eccentrics that imparted the special rocking motion

(left) Part-elevation showing the driving *lever* and pulling rod connection

An illustration from Savage's 1902 Catalogue—the caption reads, in part as follows:

'The Roundabout . . . has delighted many thousands of visitors at our English Fairs, the motion resembles the rocking of a boat at sea, and creates endless fun and amusement.'

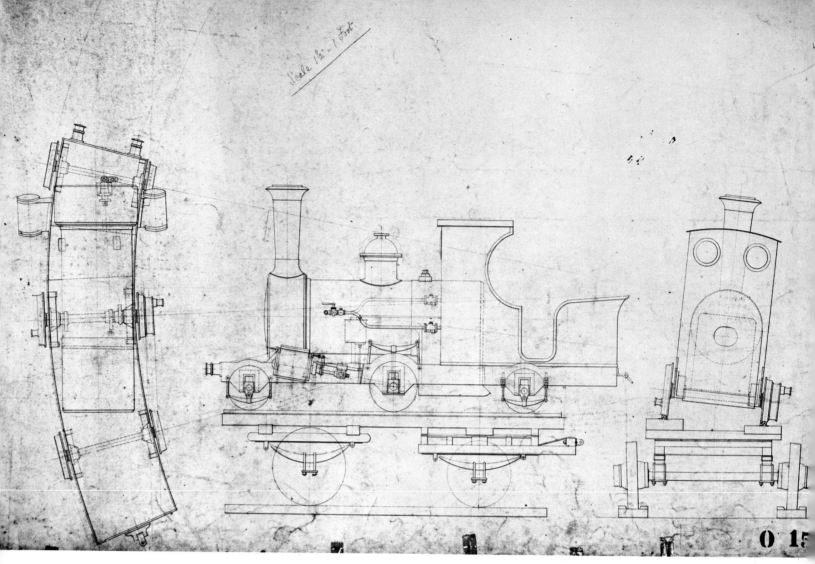

O 15

Although a departure from the principle of the spoked wheel, the very successful 'Tunnel Railway'—sometimes known as 'Channel Tunnel'—is worthy of comment. The original designer's drawing (*c.* 1885) evidences a strong French influence—the 'Sea-on-Land' was also inspired by a French roundabout. The translation of this design into mechanical and economic feasibility involved the straightening of the locomotive boiler—the original drawing showed it curved in parallel with the circular track—the provision of four additional carriages, and a tunnel which covered a complete semi-circle. Thus the train could be either fully visible or fully concealed. In addition to the locomotive two further steam engines were provided—one for generating electric light, the other driving the mechanical organ, and both discharging into a common smoke stack at the centre. The locomotive itself was a master-piece of Savage's engineering skill incorporating sand boxes and full reversing

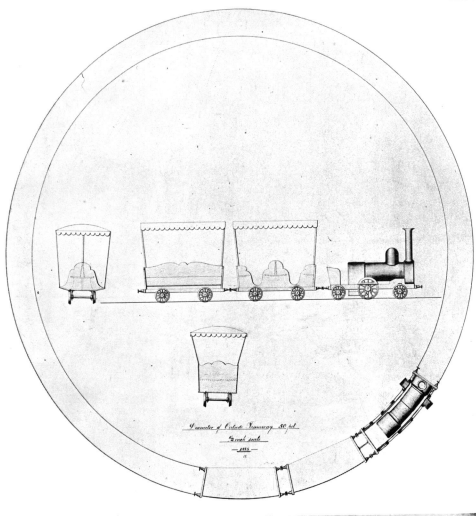

(left) The original design drawing, c. 1885, reputed to have strong French influence

(opposite page) The 'Tunnel Railway' locomotive positioned on a specially constructed road vehicle: notice the cambered track

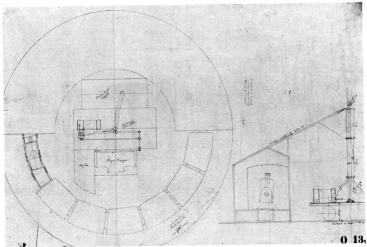

Plan and section showing the tunnel and centre assembly. The latter includes mechanical organ and engine, pay box and electric light engine. The common smoke stack also acted as centre pole

45

gear. When dismantled, a section of track mounted on a road vehicle carried the locomotive. The 'Tunnel Railway' is significant firstly in the powerful realism and excitement evoked, a railway journey being almost certainly a new experience for many at country fairs, and secondly because it reflected this contemporary transport revolution. The motor-car and aeroplane were to find expression later.

But what of the *carousel*? Most celebrated of all roundabouts, the 'Galloping Horses' derived from this, but was only mechanically possible with a steam-driven *spinning frame*. Early horse roundabouts, known as 'Dobbies', sometimes hand-propelled but also steam-driven, were being produced at King's Lynn certainly in the early 1870's, but the horses were suspended rigidly. A number of mechanisms were employed to simulate galloping motion before the overhead crank system, now common in Great Britain, appeared. 'Platform Galloping Horses' comprised a circular platform on which were pivoted large wooden horses. The driving gear was eccentric to the main carrying wheel, and the horses appeared to gallop over the platform. In 1885 Reynolds and King patented the double-crank action, a complete mechanism in which the horses were suspended and made to gallop, their legs moving independently. The success of this system was short-lived, a more rational mechanism with fewer moving parts soon replacing it. In 1886 Reynolds and King patented an even more complex roundabout in which a small locomotive with coaches ran anti-clockwise round the centre; in 1890 a machine substantially corresponding to this specification was built by Burrell's of Thetford, probably the first duo-directional roundabout ever to operate. In the same year Robert Tidman & Sons of Norwich submitted a specification for single-crank action, and with only minor modifications this system has survived all others.

The immense popularity of the 'Galloping Horse' roundabout made heavy demands on Savage's Works; the foundry and other shops expanded by leaps and bounds, and soon more than 300 men, many of them cold-iron blacksmiths, were employed. *Three-Abreast* machines were completed in three months, built up in the yard, tested and despatched. More than 30 engines were built in 1896 alone. Heavier *Four-Abreast* machines, 48 or 56 horses arranged four deep, went into production about 1890. So comprehensive were the skills of Savage's craftsmen, it was his proud boast that only two components were supplied from outside—the glass eye (the inward facing eye was carved in the wood) and tail of the horse. Bullock's tails used for this purpose were bought from the local slaughter house and split into two. In 1898 the largest set ever built—64 horses, four abreast in 16 sections—was supplied to M. Jouette in France.

A *Four-Abreast* set illustrated in the 1901 Savage catalogue was typical of

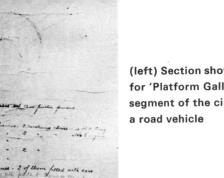

The Joy Ride

(left) Section showing *3-abreast* mounting
for 'Platform Galloping Horses'. Each
segment of the circular platform formed
a road vehicle

(below) Eccentrics on the main axle
imparted a rocking motion
The Reynolds and King 'Patent Double
Crank Galloper' at Kings Lynn Mart,
c. 1886

Fairground Architecture

(right) A children's carousel in Linnanmaki, Finland, built in Germany in 1896: notice the 'Still Horses' and counter-clockwise direction of movement

(below) Cross-section through M. Jouette's massive *4-abreast* 'Galloping Horses'—a *centre truck* designed to pass the railway loading gauge involved exceptionally high trams

(opposite page)

1 *4-abreast* set illustrated in Savage's 1902 Catalogue

2 A Belgian 'Still Horse' roundabout

3 'Lead Horse' on McCullough's Carousel, Coney Island, New York

4 George Irvin & Sons' 'Galloping Horses'

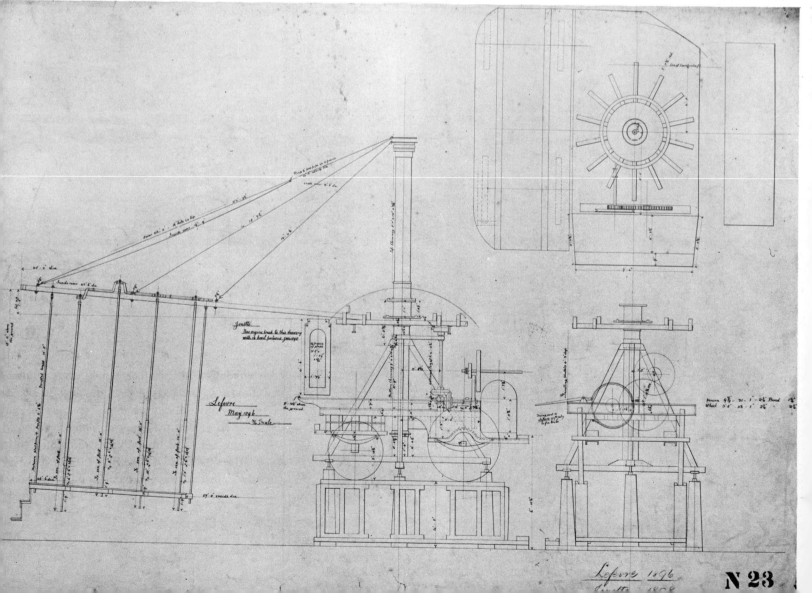

N 23

the high standard of craftsmanship. Because of the increased speeds a 'swinging out' motion was devised—it was incorporated in this set. The *horse rods* extended below the platform, passing through radial slots. As the speed increased, both rider and horse were free to swing out to about 15 degrees.

Many of the finest 'Galloping Horse' roundabouts have disappeared and others have fallen into disrepair, but after a period when the switchback and other rides held sway the popularity of the 'Horses' has returned—this time as a novelty ride. Today about 70 sets are still in use—one-third of them are on tour. 'Still Horse' roundabouts remain popular in France, Holland, Belgium and the United States, but in all these countries they rotate counter-clockwise with the sun. Only on British roundabouts can the horse be mounted from the correct side—a tradition which surely stems from a right-handed swordsman being able to mount his steed without discomfort.

1

2

3

4

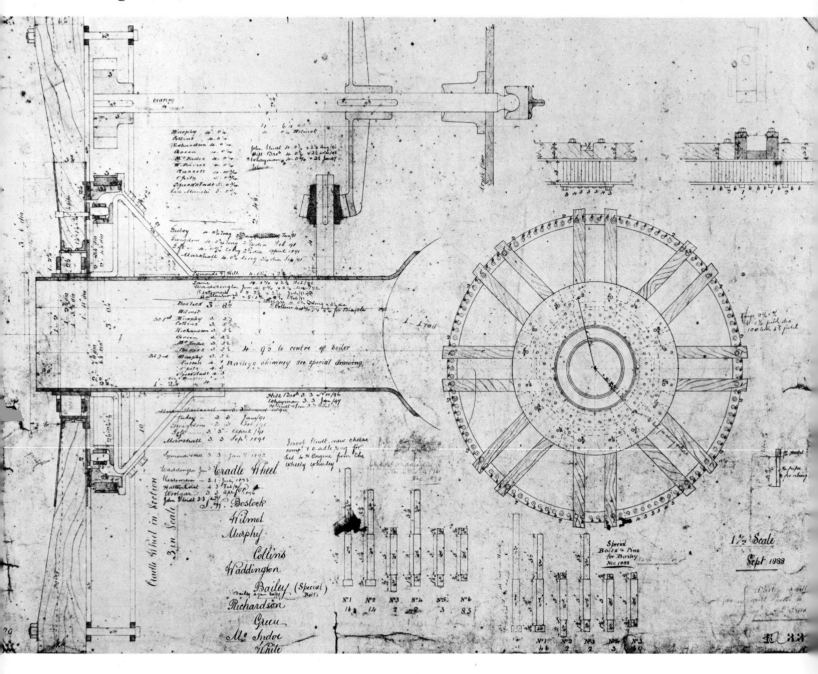

Original drawing of the centre *cheese* or *cradle* wheel developed by Frederick Savage for the switchback—the number of showmen listed attests the success of this invention

The circular switchback, as originally conceived, had two hills and two valleys in a track of 40 ft diameter. Eight cars coupled together were driven round the undulating track by a *spinning frame*. Despite the improvisations of a perambulator manufacturer, and Messrs. Marshall and Waddington of Leeds, the cars invariably left the track on ascending the hills. While Tidman, Reynolds and King were busy devising ' galloping horse ' systems Frederick Savage was designing a switchback which incorporated a third compensating rail, an ingenious idea to prevent derailment. The idea proved successful, and Savage took out patents in 1888. By 1904 more than 40 switchbacks had been built at King's Lynn and some of them were exported. A special telegraphic code was instituted for overseas customers thus:—'CARRIAL VERTICAL TRUMPET QUEENLY ' represented 'Switchback Roundabout—8 hp centre engine with vertical organ engine and trumpet organ. We can ship in three months '.

George Aspland's 'Venetian Gondola' switchback illustrated in Savage's 1902 Catalogue

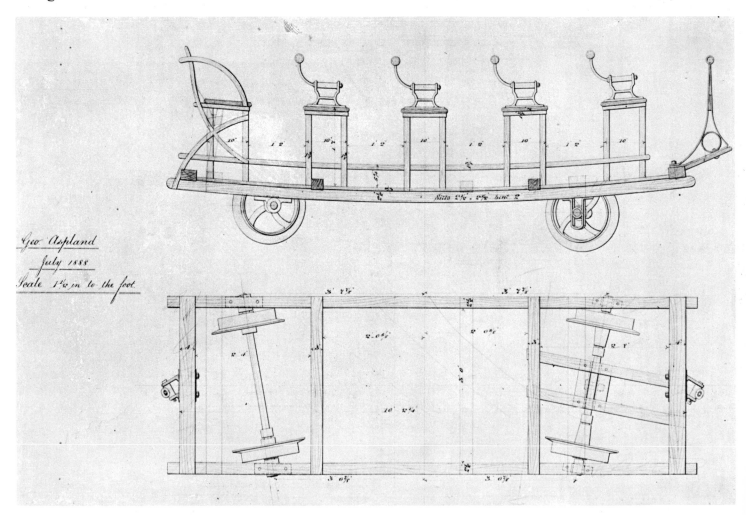

Geo Aspland
July 1888
Scale 1½ in to the foot

Detail of an early switchback car built for
George Aspland in July, 1888

(right) John Green's 'Toastrack' switchback
on Accrington Market Place, 1889: notice
the *Spinning Top* and second platform
for spectators

The earlier examples were not, however, so elaborate as the original drawing of Aspland's switchback car shows.

A more powerful centre engine was required to drive the switchback, and it was mounted on a gantry truck, the boiler raised to a height of 7 ft above ground level. Although this was an awkward arrangement its concealment offered more surface area for high relief carvings. Unlike the 'Galloping Horses' the build-up involved setting out radial sleepers to carry the track, a difficult task on uneven ground as they had to be levelled.

Because of the profuse decorations the switchback soon became known as the 'Scenic Railway', and cars which were carved, gilded, and inset with cut glass mirrors were called *gondolas*. The rolling and pitching motion, used first in the 'Sea-on-Land' machine, was adapted to give the *gondola* an exciting rocking action. Later, *gondolas* were replaced by dummy motor-cars.

George Twigdon's 'Gondola' switchback photographed in Derbyshire in 1904. This *machine* **was later sold to William Thurston**

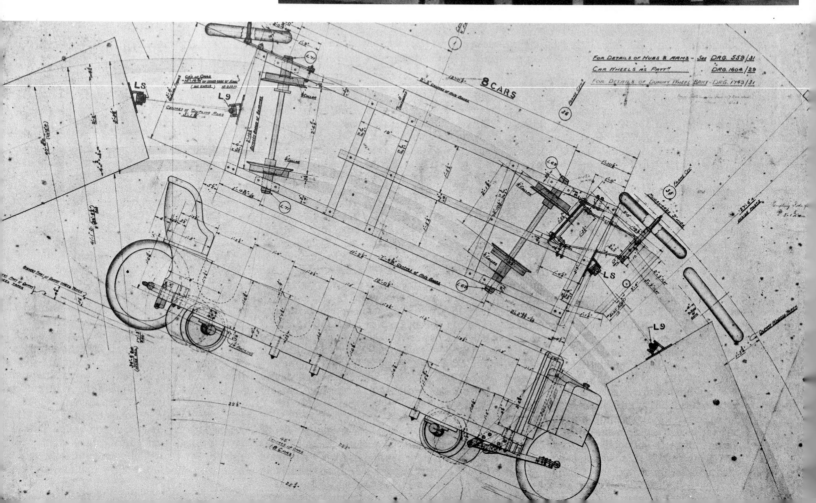

(left) Enoch Farrar's 'Dragon Scenic' in Grantham, 1921. This fine *machine* was built by George Orton, Sons & Spooner Limited of Burton-on-Trent—the organ was a 98-key Gaudin

(below left) Detail of a *motor-car* specially designed to replace the ornate and now dated *gondola*

Percy Cole's 'Venetian Gondolas'—formerly Aspland's—and only recently converted to electric-drive

Initially rating second in popularity to the 'Gallopers', the 'Scenic Railway' attained a higher point in terms of fairground architecture. Italian designers and craftsmen were specially imported, and to many showmen expense was apparently no object. Reconstruction of Leon Steppe's machine, described later, was reputed to have cost between £8,000 and £9,000. The centre piece was always a mechanical organ, the epitome of exuberance, a miracle of mechanical ingenuity crowned with an ornate proscenium.

Around 1910 electric traction was introduced, and direct conduction through the rails obviated the need for a centre engine and, for that matter, the *spinning frame*. Motors of five horse-power rating were fitted under each car, and with the centre engine removed more space was available for scenery. Thus the *scenic centre* evolved. Larger organs, salvaged from the 'Bioscope Shows' which are referred to in a later chapter, were installed, fountains played, and special lighting effects abounded. But 50 tons or so of high and low relief, miscellaneous statuary and diverse mechanical effects constituted a heavy pay load and required a large staff for assembly and dismantling, and consequently the era of the 'Scenic' was brief. All too ephemeral were Goldthorpe Marshall's 'Proud Peacocks' and Fred Cox's 'Father Neptune Scenic'. High speed lightweight machines, like the 'Noah's Ark' or 'Ben Hur Speedway' introduced in the late 1920's and the 'Autodrome' in the 1930's have taken their place. One Savage-built machine remains—Percy Cole's 'Venetian Gondolas'; although still on tour, it is now very much a museum piece.

The unlikely partnership of musician and mechanical engineer, Henry Cracknell and William Cartwright, patented a steam swing in 1888. The swinging motion was imparted by connecting rod, and a special trip gear was incorporated to prevent the piston from over-running dead centre. This trip gear became known as the *rabbit* because of its basic shape, and was probably copied from a contemporary threshing machine. A hand gear-lever at the side of the firebox operated the slide valve for starting up, and great concentration was called for—if the driver neglected to set the slide valve for the next upward stroke a cylinder explosion could occur with lethal consequences. In 1894 Frederick Savage built a set of two swings, later to become known as 'Steam Yachts', with a more advanced portable engine arranged between them. The motion was by chain drive and the setting of the slide was automatic once the yachts were in motion. The remarkable speed of 14 cycles per minute was achieved.

Only a limited number of 'Steam Yachts' was built, and now they are very rare indeed. Of the two or three sets still on tour the finest example belongs to Harry Lee, a Yorkshire showman. Mr. Lee's set was delivered new to King's

Lynn Mart in 1901, and has been carefully preserved in more or less original condition—only the engine has been replaced.

The ' Big Wheel ' has probably been in existence as long as roundabouts and swings, and its development has been limited to expansion and refinement. Peter Mundy records as follows:—' . . . like a crane wheel at the Custom House Quay and turned in that manner, whereon children set on little seats hung round about in several parts thereof. . . ' Stumpy wooden frames were replaced, first by steel, then by aluminium alloy. Cars are freely pivoted so as to remain always horizontal—this has always been the case—but the drive is now by continuous cable channelled round the perimeter and passed over a tensioning pulley and driving pulley at the base. Otherwise basic design principles have remained unchanged for more than a century. The ' Great Wheel ' at the Earls Court Exhibition in 1894, a semi-permanent structure, seated 1,200 riders in 40 carriages. The diameter measured 280 ft and two 50 hp engines were used to drive it.

There have been many variants of the ' Big Wheel '—' Sky Wheels ', ' Paratrooper ' and ' Flying Saucers ' are recent ones—and some have been as fabulous as their inventors, who include an Italian Crown Consul. This latter gentleman devised a ride in miniature *wheels* that were made to cascade down

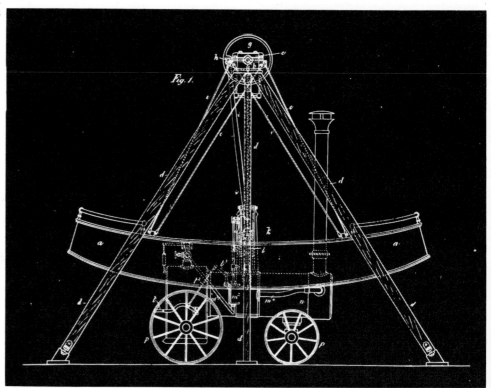

Henry Cartwright and William Cracknell's patent 'Steam Swing' 1888—Cartwright's later chain-drive version (1894) differed only slightly in general arrangement

Mr Harry Lee's 'Steam Yachts' Columbia & Shamrock

Built by Savage Brothers of Kings Lynn, Norfolk 1901

DRAWN BY DAVID BRAITHWAITE

Harry Lee's Savage-built 'Steam Yachts'
at the Great Steam Fair, White Waltham,
in 1964

Harry Lee's 'Steam Yachts' at Stratford-
upon-Avon—also in 1964

Capstan-drive 'Big Wheels' at a Fair in St. Petersburg, c. 1804

the spiral chute of an enormous 'Helter Skelter'. Small *wheels* replaced round-about cars, a device invented by F. W. Allchin of Northampton and resurrected in the late 1940's as the 'Looper'. But none has met with great success—the time lag in loading and unloading individual cars has always inhibited profitable operation.

Four years before his death in 1897, Savage patented the 'Razzle Dazzle', otherwise known as 'Whirligig' or 'Aerial Novelty'. A circular platform, mounted high on the centre pole with seats arranged radially, was made to tilt up and down as it revolved. Described by veteran showmen as 'a good oncer'— that is, a ride the *punters* would normally go on once—and once only—this must have been the least successful of his inventions. But modern rides like the 'Octopus', 'Meteorite' and 'Satellite' owe a great deal to this odd machine.

Contemporary, more or less, with the Edison Bell phonograph, there

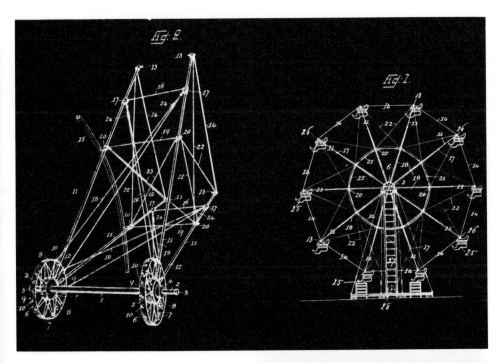

(above) A demountable steel-framed
'Big Wheel' patented by Crist in 1902

(right) 'Big Wheel' at Mitcham Fair, 1966

The 'Great Wheel' at the Earls Court
Exhibition of 1894

Building-up the 'Looper' at Mitcham Fair, 1966

The underworks of Harry Holland's 'Cakewalk' photographed at Nottingham in 1958. In the earlier *machines* belt-drive for a mechanical organ would come from this remarkable piece of industrial archaeology. The faster the organ played —the quicker the patrons danced—and, inevitably, the better the takings

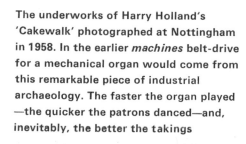

emerged the 'Cakewalk' or 'Dancing Machine'. With banners describing it as 'Captivating', 'Invigorating', 'Rejuvenating', 'Progressive British Sport', this machine was unique, and perhaps reflected the spirit of the times more than any other. Patentee Herbert Alfred Lawson, an art master from Cleethorpes, described it thus:—[the] ' machine consists of a number of mechanical waves formed by a series of hinged bridges or gangways . . . the ends of which alternately rise and fall . . . to be used as a form of amusement by persons either walking or dancing along the bridges . . . the whole machine is actuated by one crank giving a circular motion to the ends of the bridges, causing the whole of the series of waves to reciprocate a distance limited by the throw of the crank . . . Persons either walking or dancing . . . are subjected to the same motions as the surface of the machine.' A ' Figure-8 Cakewalk ' built by Thos. Walker of Tewkesbury is described as follows: ' This Machine causes

John Collin's Razzle Dazzle', c. 1900

'Razzle Dazzle' at Newcastle Town Moor
Fair, c. 1906

C. W. Parker's patent 'Balloon Roundabout' 1888

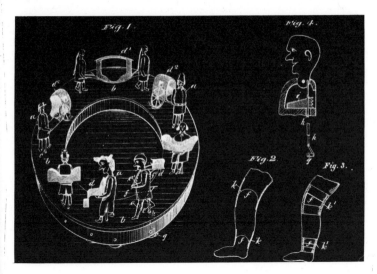

H. P. Jackson's 'Waltzing Dolls', 1920

a lot of frolic and amusement owing to the antics made by the Passengers in their passage of the Moving Gangways.' Of the half-dozen or so ' Cakewalks ' still on tour, the most popular belongs to the Bishton family, Nottingham-shire and Derbyshire travellers.

The 19th century was a fertile period in the development of the joyride, and most of the basic forms were evolved, at least in embryo, by 1900. The main stream of development has been traced, but there were many highly individual rides—a political roundabout, with Conservative and Liberal Um-brellas a panoramic ' Joy Wheel ' using kinetoscope effects to create the illusion of a race between motor-car and train, and then there was a steam-driven ' See-Saw ' designed to carry 100 persons. There were also some gro-tesque *waltzing dolls*, later scaled up larger than life, pirouetting on a revolving platform, carrying baskets, sedan chairs and the like, for humans to ride in.

The Industrial Revolution gave impetus, exuberance, and a high degree of sophistication to the roundabout builders. Momentous engineering achieve-ments in the 1880's and 1890's were paralleled by irrepressible mechanical ingenuity in the amusements industry. In a generation that produced the Forth Bridge, the first electric power stations, Daimler's motor-car and Bell's telephone, there emerged Thwaite's ' Gravity Pleasure Railway ', the ' Sea-on-Land ' roundabout, a ' Balloon roundabout ', to say nothing of illuminated ' Galloping Horses ', ' Dragons ' breathing artificial fire, and the ' Tunnel of Love '. With the roundabout as its pivot the Pleasure Fair was the effer-vescence and sparkle of a period of ruthless and unrelenting manufacture.

Fairground Architecture

The ever popular 'Coconut Shy'

The *Great Italian Annual Fair*—an 18th Century painting by Teniers

BOOTHS AND JOINTS

As long as there have been surplus goods to sell—that is, as long as the merchant class has existed—there have been booths to shelter both goods and vendor. The random assembly of *portables and fit-ups* that characterised the fair before the Industrial Revolution has been sensitively portrayed in contemporary paintings. With the commercial boom however, display became an essential adjunct to shelter and, as a result, decorations and enticing slogans began to appear. From this time forward a hundred years or so witnessed the transformation from anonymous *four posters* to the ornate 'Electric Bioscope'.

A social revolution was implicit, too. Trading at some of the larger fairs began to decline in the latter part of the 17th century. The coming of railways eclipsed all but the horse fair, but a concurrent transition from trading to pleasure did more than perpetuate the fair. To many events it brought vitality, a new lease of life. The 'Goose Fair' at Nottingham, a name given to the Michaelmas Fair already established at the time of Edward I's charter in 1284, was a trading fair of only average importance. As a pleasure fair it rates as the best event of the year.

The spirit of competition, much in evidence at mediæval tournaments and tilting matches, pervaded the fairground too. Games of chance and of skill made their appearance long before the roundabout. According to Muncey, London's May Fair, instituted by James II in 1689, had boxing matches, ass racing, dice tables, hasty-pudding-eaters and eel divers, and the Frost Fair was famous for its horse and coach races. Because of local characteristics and the spontaneous nature of such diversions it is impossible to set out a precise history, and the *joints* that gave them shelter were probably just as spontaneous. By 1900, however, fairground planning and the emergent structure of ground rentals led to co-ordination of the plan form at least.

Joints fall into roughly three categories—round ones, generically termed *hoop-las*, *side-stuff*, measured as frontage, and casual stalls for vending. Side-shows, four poster and six poster, vary in depth according to the game enclosed—bottle shooters are always longer than darts—and frontage depends on either the number of players or the space actually available. Directional games, involving throwing a ball or shooting a rifle, are the most common side-show—they usually have painted boards announcing the name of the showman and scenic prosceniums are not uncommon. Striped awnings, embroidered side linings, and *swag* stands, complete the basic shell, but embellishments to the game itself predominate. *Round-uns* often incorporate a brightly-painted shutter, waist-high, to prevent unfair leaning over, and the division into radial segments for individual players gives scope for imaginative decoration and display. Where a revolving feature appears, full advantage is taken of suitable roundabout motifs. But vending stalls have retained a charm of their own because of their haphazard placing and the sometimes accidental nature of their structure.

There is in fact a close affinity between the market trader's stall and the side-show. More than just the garish display of *swag* (prizes), it is this quality of jostling for space, of being smarter than one's neighbour. The sheer size and power of the roundabouts demand obeisance—lighting and modes of decoration reflected—but in terms of intimacy, tangibility of the goods displayed and the persuasive voice and gesture of the pitch-getter, *joints* must clearly be regarded as separate artifacts.

The booth, on the other hand, was essentially a static shelter enclosing both audience and performer, excluding daylight. Decoration was concentrated on the show front, and to a minor degree on the proscenium within. Shows that are termed *walk-up* derived from the raised platform where musicians and performers paraded to draw the crowds. With the beating of drums and clamour of bells, would-be spectators mounted the platform, paid their money, and then descended into the booth.

With the romantic urges of the working man seeking out more sophisticated forms of entertainment, miracle plays, a legacy from the Middle Ages, were now presented as elaborate spectacles. The companies of Richardson, Hancock and Saunders travelled far and wide and for a time drama was respectable.

Hatwell Brother's 'Royal African Jungle Shooter' at Stratford-upon-Avon Mop Fair, 1961

Billy Mayne's 'Wheel 'Em In' at the Great Steam Fair, White Waltham, 1964

J. Mayne's 'Roll Ups' at the Great Steam Fair, White Waltham, 1964

WOMBWELL'S
Royal Menagerie,
GREAT ACCESSION OF NOVELTY.

IN consequence of the engagement of the stupendous **SIAMESE ROYAL ELEPHANT** being about to be fulfilled the Proprietor has great satisfaction in thus noticing that the **TWO ELE-PHANTS,** (Male and Female, the first instance of the kind ever known in these countries,) which he has but just imported are arrived and exhibiting in the Menagerie, as also **FIVE ROYAL TIGERS,** which by the same conveyance reached this Town from his DEPOT IN LONDON; a Survey of the Menagerie as it is now stocked can not fail, to give universal satisfaction, delight, and instruction.

The Menagerie will remain in Town for a few Days next Week.

J. Clark, Printer, 11, Newgate Street, Newcastle

Wombwell's wild beast show—a contemporary poster

Even the great Henry Fielding had a booth. But in 1697, and again in 1700, stage plays were suppressed at Bartholomew Fair. Puppet plays too suffered much the same fate, oddly enough because the authorities were more than a little disturbed by their satirical content.

Coincident with the first presentations of drama, *c.* 1500, were the first wild beast shows. ' Educational Exhibitions ' so-called, these travelling menageries were basically unwholesome, and cruel sports like bear-baiting and dog-and-lion fights were practised. Curiosity, that can only be qualified as morbid, was a quality much exploited by the showmen. For example, the untimely death of Wombwell's elephant en route to Bartholomew Fair was surprisingly turned to good effect. Banners on a rival booth proclaimed ' the only live elephant in the fair '—Wombwell retaliated with ' the only dead elephant in the fair ', and drew far greater crowds.

Nevertheless wild beast shows enjoyed great popularity in the 18th and 19th centuries. The name of Pidcock is among the earliest on record (about 1708). The Nottingham Journal of 28th September 1805 lists the following attractions at Polito's show, mentioned in an earlier chapter:—

a lion, striped Bengal tiger and tigress,
four kangaroos from Botany Bay,
panthers, beaver, leopard and leopardess,
wolves from the Alps, and muscovy cats.

Later the names of Bostock and Wombwell, Atkins and Chipperfield were prominent, and their respective shows were less gory and therefore, especially from the animals' point of view, much healthier.

In addition to primitive and savage spectacles involving animals, there were many death-defying human acts. Prior to her marriage to the first Lord George Sanger, Pauline de Vere used to put her head in a lion's mouth as the climax of her act. Less skilful performers were, alas, unable to keep their heads. But equestrian acts, like *haute école*, the result of intense training and proficient horsemanship, with techniques dating back to tournaments and jousting, were also brought to the fairground. Soon these were to merge with the wire dancers, tumblers, jugglers and clowns, to form the rich fabric of the circus.

Curiosity was also a prime factor in the success of the peep show. Intensely private in its enjoyment, a flood of optical inventions in the 18th and 19th centuries brought great improvements. Depicting the Battle of Trafalgar, the show presented by Lord George Sanger had 26 glasses for 26 viewers, and the pictures, illuminated by a row of tallow candles, were pulled up and down by strings. An Irishman, usually intoxicated, painted the scenes for him—with plenty of strong colour—for 3/6; battle pieces with plentiful corpses ran to 7/6.

Fair Time—a painting by Paul Meyerheim

(top) Patrick Collin's 'Great Wonderland
Bioscope Show' with mammoth 110-key
organ—Nottingham Goose Fair, 1913

Frontispiece from Gavioli & Co's. Organ
Catalogue (right) Three Gavioliphones
from the Catalogue

(top right) 89-key Gavioli (1904) formerly
in Crighton's 'Bioscope Show' now
preserved by Mr. W. G. Chamberlain

(bottom right) 89-key Gavioli (1895)
formerly in Peters' 'Golden Gallopers'
now preserved by Mr. D. Robinson

Magic lantern shows, the phanatascope, zöetrope and kinetoscope followed, culminating in the beginnings of cinema—the ' Bioscope '.

In the days of horse transport, cinema shows were staged in ground booths, according to Arthur Fay in his book *Bioscope Shows and their Engines*. These booths had no front stage or steps, and a pay box was erected on the ground. Timber shutters formed the sides, and a dark canvas *tilt* excluded most of the light. There was no seating for the audience of 50 or so, and the beam from the projector scarcely cleared the heads of those in front. Light for the projector came from cylinders of oxygen and hydrogen, the lighted hydrogen being first directed on to a cone of lime—thus it was literally *limelight*. Then the oxygen was turned on gradually.

It was not until the showman's road locomotive came into general usage that the two-wagon fronted shows appeared. Then the ' Bioscope Show ' attained a high point in terms of fairground architecture, just as the ' Scenic ' was to do 10 or 20 years later; both had the same element—the mammoth organ.

Mechanical organs were first imported to this country in the late 1870's; their principal use was then in roundabouts. But with more elaborate show fronts, more emphasis on the parade, Gavioli ' Orchestrophones ' began to replace small bands of perhaps not very adept musicians. Competition between showmen demanded bigger and better organs, more elaborate carving, more dazzling lighting effects, and so on. Whereas the ground booth would have only a hand-turned trumpet barrel organ, the mature ' Bioscope ', glorying in names like ' Palace of Light ', ' Wonderland ' and ' Royal Electrograph ', would have massive 110-key organs.

Ludovic Gavioli was the greatest of all organ builders. He established a workshop in Paris in 1845, and for more than half a century built mechanical organs of superb quality. Around 1892, Anselme Gavioli introduced the book system for playing the organs, a system which superseded the costly hand-pinned roller or cylinder. The book system used perforated cardboard pages, flexibly jointed, which passed through a pneumatically-operated key frame. This Gavioli invention resulted in reduced costs and increased repertoire. One hundred yards of music were given free with every organ, and thereafter the cost pro rata was about 4/- per yard. But the Gaviolis were not good business men, and in the early 1900's the factory closed. Charles Marenghi, their foreman, started his own factory and built many fine organs complete with magnificent prosceniums. After his death in 1919, the Gaudin brothers carried on the business for a few years.

Savages of King's Lynn supplied a number of portable electric light engines to ' Bioscope ' owners, but they built only one or two wagon fronts. It was to Orton, Sons and Spooner of Burton-upon-Trent that most of the Gavioli

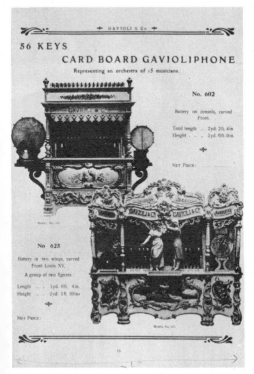

and Marenghi organs went. There they were built into road trucks, elaborate show-fronts added and hinged shutters fitted. The lowered shutters formed the platform. A canvas awning above, carved and gilded pay boxes, the electric light engine, or traction engine, and steps with ornate balustrading, completed the facade. Arthur Fay describes Mrs. Holland's ' Palace of Light ' thus:—

' In the Palace of Light was seating accommodation for six hundred people with standing room in the gallery for another four hundred. The seating was upholstered in Italian green figured cloth with backs to match, while the side linings were of heavy blue figured plush trimmed and ornamented with gold tassels, as also were the side door curtains. From the inside top lining, which was of red and gold, were suspended sixteen Japanese lampshades (eight down either side of the ceiling) in pink and gold '.

With these beautiful show fronts illuminated by *golden flame* electric arc lamps, and powerful spotlights playing on the dancing girls, it is perhaps not surprising that the crowds had to be held back forcibly. But the era of the ' Bioscope ' soon passed—the declaration of war in 1914, followed later by the establishing of permanent cinemas in most towns, brought an abrupt halt. By good fortune some of the organs have been preserved, transferred to electric ' Scenics ', but the excitement of animated picture shows under canvas with all that this involved—the parade, the organ, the dazzling lights—had gone for ever.

Boxing Pavilions and freak shows have survived the rigours of time, but not so travelling ' Wax Works ' like that of Mrs. Jarley's so minutely observed by Charles Dickens in *The Old Curiosity Shop*. 'Wild West' shows and *glamour shows* like the ' Naughty Nineties Revue ' are recent innovations. The parade and show front have not disappeared altogether, but the spectacle is now more tawdry than lavish.

(right) An early 'Bioscope Show', c. 1897, owned by Simons and photographed in North Wales

(below right) John Proctor's 'Royal Bioscope' on tour in Nottinghamshire in the early 1900s

A portable show front built by Savage Brothers Limited on tow by one of the firm's 'Little Samson' steam tractor

UP TO DATE CINEMATOGRAPH

A 'Variety Show' at Nottingham Goose
Fair in the late 1950s

(below left and bottom) Jack Gage's Boxing
Booth at Oxford St. Giles Fair, 1966

(below) A line up of shows at Nottingham
Goose Fair, 1965

TRANSPORTATION

A good deal of nonsense is talked about the open road, but in the early days, for showmen travelling between fairs, there were many adventures—often there were mishaps, sometimes disaster. The race to secure good positions on the *tober* led to fierce rivalry between the horse-drawn road trains. Their inability to pass one another on pre-Macadam roads often led to open warfare, with wild beasts escaping and running amok to terrorize the unfortunate farmers and villagers. The journey from Nottingham Goose Fair to Hull, usually the second week-end in October and still a desperate rush today, has, for this reason, a dramatic history.

The means of transportation remained of secondary importance until the commercial expansion that followed the Industrial Revolution. Then, as already stressed, the roundabout business really boomed. Engineering skills inherent in the machines demanded new techniques in erecting and dismantling, and the speed of travel from town to town became increasingly important. Components were numbered and soon a new science of wagon building evolved, with compartments formed to precise dimensions. In this way the sequence of packing and unpacking, and therefore the ordered system of building-up and dismantling, became very much a precision routine. Economy in packing was important, too, because the fewer the loads the fewer the horses that were required.

Fairground Architecture

A Savage-built electric light engine generating for James Hibbert's 'Galloper' (Reproduced by courtesy of the British Fairground Society)

(opposite page top) *En route* from Burnopfield to Rowlands Gill in County Durham, the engine and first trailer broke the rails and plunged 40 ft. into Park Dene—the driver was killed (May 1923)

(opposite page below) An accident at Wooler Bridge, Northumberland, c. 1908—Wilson's Fowler engine 'Dawn of the Century' in serious trouble

(below) Sedgwick's Menagerie on the move

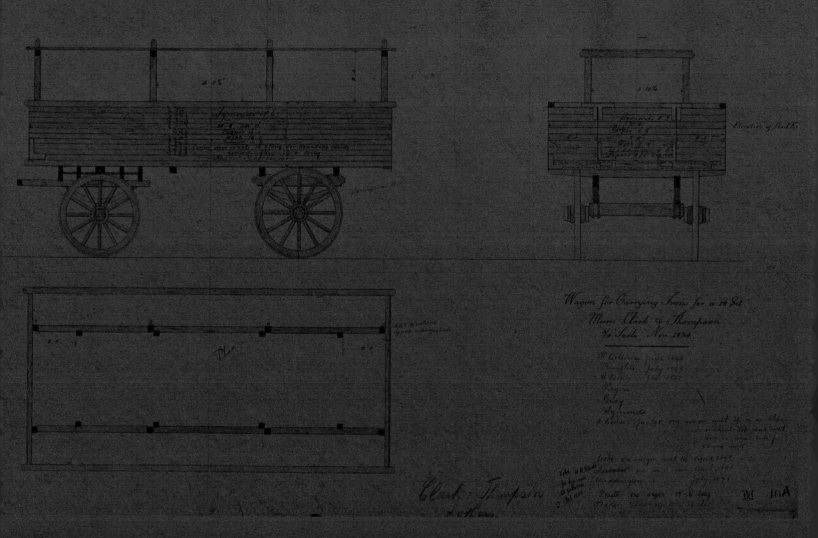

A wagon specially built by Savages of Kings Lynn for packing *horse irons* and the like

The centre truck with its engine was inevitably very heavy, and steep hills necessitated doubling up the horses. The alternative of rail transport still involved using horses from rail-head to fairground, but despite this a number of centre trucks were built to the railway loading gauge. Electric light engines were heavy, too, and this factor delayed the widespread use of electricity on the fairground.

The problem of weight was perhaps even more acute with travelling menageries. In the early 1880's Wombwell's first show had 14 wagons drawn by 50 to 60 horses. The elephant wagon, 30 ft long and 9 ft wide, with full payload weighed more than 8 tons. The width of each of the six wheels measured 18 ins and 30 good horses were needed on up-gradients. Feeble canal bridges had to be propped before the elephant wagon could pass over, and punitive tolls were extracted from the showmen.

With great skill, Frederick Savage, the master roundabout builder at King's Lynn, produced packing trucks to carry the *swifts* (spokes), *irons*, *horses* and *roundings*. The *three-abreast* machine was reduced to three loads, plus organ, and the following meticulous schedule was drawn up by Savage's firm for shipping the ' Colonial Horses ':—

' Centre Engine and Truck	$14'\,0'' \times 7'\,6'' \times 5'\,0''$	525 cu ft
1 Bundle of Trams	$13'\,0'' \times 1'\,0'' \times 0'\,6''$	6 ,, ,,
3 Packing Cases, each	$3'\,0'' \times 2'\,0'' \times 1'\,0''$	18 ,, ,,
2 Bundles of Swifts, each	$17'\,0'' \times 2'\,0'' \times 1'\,6''$	102 ,, ,,
4 Bundles of Quarterings, each	$9'\,0'' \times 2'\,0'' \times 0'\,6''$	36 ,, ,,
2 Bundles of Rounding Boards, each	$9'\,0'' \times 3'\,0'' \times 2'\,0''$	108 ,, ,,
1 Crown Centre	$5'\,0'' \times 3'\,6'' \times 2'\,0''$	35 ,, ,,
1 Bundle Tilt Rods	$11'\,0'' \times 1'\,0'' \times 0'\,6''$	55 ,, ,,
2 Bundles Horse Irons, each	$11'\,6'' \times 1'\,0'' \times 1'\,0''$	23 ,, ,,
18 Crates of Horses (2 in each), each	$5'\,6'' \times 2'\,0'' \times 3'\,0''$	594 ,, ,,
	Total cubic feet	1,502 ,, ,,

Centre truck for a steam-drive 'Dobby' set built by Thomas Walker of Tewkesbury

Approximate shipping weight 37 tons .'

A showman's 'Scenic' engine built by Charles Burrell & Sons Limited of Thetford—now owned in preservation and shown here at the Castle Howard Steam Fair, 1965

The centre truck and centre engine have already been discussed in Chapter 3, *The Joy Ride*. The centre assembly for 'Gallopers' is substantially the same, excepting that *top motion* gear (to actuate the cranks) is mounted above the *cheese*. In the 1890's, however, the steam road locomotive began to replace the horses, and perhaps because of the immense tractive effort thereby released the surface area and weight of decoration increased sharply. Early in the 1890's heavy *three-abreast* 'Gallopers' went into production, and around 1892 the *four-abreast* machine was introduced.

Without the road locomotive neither switchback nor steam swing could have been transported, but the heavy wagons created a new problem of overheating axles and the consequent danger of fire. And there was the hazard, too, of core plugs blowing between streams. Fetching and carrying the water to top up the boiler could mean a delay of half-a-day, and this in turn could result in

Charles Thurston's Burrell 'Victory' with jib attached. In 1947, when surplus machinery owned by the Thurston family was put up for auction, 'Victory' fetched only £28. Today it is owned by Mr. George Cushing of Laurel Farm, Thursford, Norfolk

missing a fair altogether.

The first engine built by Charles Burrell & Sons of Thetford and used by a showman was 'Monarch' (No. 1451). According to records contained in *Chronicles of a Country Works* by Ronald H. Clark, the engine was exhibited at Smithfield Show in 1889 and on the 21st December it was despatched to Jacob Studt of Pontypridd. With spoked flywheel, half cab and no dynamo it bore little resemblance to the mature 'Scenic' engine.

There were special qualities about the purpose-made showman's engine which distinguished it from the more commonplace haulage or agricultural engine. Unique design parameters included the requirement to have a dynamo mounted in front of the smoke box and a crane to lift the roundabout cars, but equally functional as far as the showman was concerned were the brass embellishments and painted decoration—the general livery, in fact. The visual

DRAWING № 711

DRAWER № 30

(left) A wagon purpose-built for packing four switchback *gondolas*

(right) The portable engine for Walter Ling's 'Steam Yachts'—build-up at Nottingham Goose Fair, 1958. This set formerly belonged to Harry Gray of London.

(below) An original works drawing of the remarkable *traction centre* engine 'Empress' (1898)

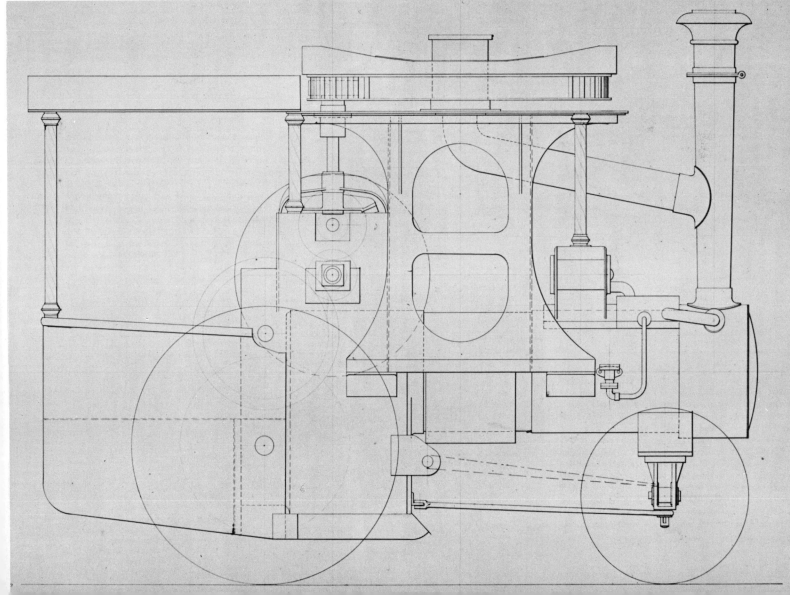

Fairground Architecture

This fine engine was built in 1917 by John Fowler & Co. Limited of Leeds for the Ministry of Munitions. In 1919 showman Jacob Studt purchased the engine—no doubt at bargain price—for it was then upside down after an accident on Birdlip Hill. Rebuilt as a showman's engine, the names 'Prince of Wales', 'Excelsior' and 'Birdlip' preceded the present one 'Evening Star'. Photographed here at the Great Steam Fair, Little Waltham, 1964, the present owners are M. D. Thackray & Sons, Old Malton, Yorkshire.

John W. Hoadley's Scammell 'Showtrac'

(above left) L. C. Byass & Son's Burrell 'Success' at Castle Howard Steam Fair, 1965

(left) W. H. Dorman's Burrell 'Dreadnought' formerly owned by showman Albert Holland and travelled in the Midlands.

impact of engine and loads in transit was never under-estimated.

Burrell's incorporated the following items as standard specification for 'Scenic' engines: an organ whistle mounted on the cylinders, full length awning (cab) supported on six twisted brass columns, brass stars and rings to the side plates, brass stars to the cylinder covers, brass ring to the flywheel, brass axle caps, and brass segmented name plate in front of the dynamo platform. Although crimson with yellow wheels was the most popular colour scheme, Tuby of Doncaster had two royal blue engines. 'Wait and See', an engine built for Crowther and Johnson, was pale yellow, lined with crimson, green and black, and the wheels were white, lined with red and blue.

In 1898 Savage built a remarkable engine known as the *traction centre*. A turret to carry the *spinning top* was built up from the boiler and an auxiliary flue diverted smoke through an extended centre pole. The drive was by dog clutch and bevel gears off the crankshaft. But an engine powerful enough to draw a road train of 40 tons was a good deal too powerful to drive a roundabout. All too often the *swifts* would snap and riders and platforms fall to the ground. Needless to say, the *traction centre* enjoyed little success.

The switchback was altogether a heavier machine and consequently involved a longer road train. Packing trucks were specially designed to carry four cars—*gondolas*. With two such trucks, plus the centre and organ trucks, at least two further wagons were required for 'loose stuff'—sub-frames, *gates* and shutters, *roundings* and so on. Steam swings were scarcely less awkward with the two *boats* each requiring a truck, the portable engine, an organ, and loose stuff. But the electric 'Scenic', replete with deep *rounding boards*, extension front, 'Bioscope' organ and elaborate centre assembly constituted the heaviest pay load ever and often required the attendance of two traction engines. Economics eventually forced them off the road, and by 1930 when the £60 annual licence for showmen's engines was introduced the era was substantially over.

By comparison with the railway locomotive, showmen's engines never attained a high level of technological optimisation. Massive driving wheels, dynamo and deep cab remained to the end. With the need to take on water every eight miles or so, and a maximum speed of around 15 mph, there were obvious disadvantages, yet these were more than compensated for by the aggressively powerful machine aesthetic. According to Clark, one of the best times ever set up was from King's Lynn to Downham Market—11 miles in exactly one hour with the loads of a full cinematograph show.

The firm of Pat Collins, who in their heyday had more than 30 engines licensed, were still using the Foster 'The Leader' in 1958. Through the praiseworthy efforts of enthusiasts many of these fine engines have been preserved. Apart from the brief era of the 'Showtrac' diesel tractor no other vehicles have been specially designed for showmen.

B. Peter's Living van

The parlour in W

(below) **A showman's living van illustrated in Savage Brother's 1902 Catalogue**

(bottom) **Bostock and Wombwell's Menagerie on the Great North Road, 1913—three loads plus water butt with a more temperamental prime mover**

(right) **The build-up at Mitcham Fair in the 1920s**

(above left) A living van of the present generation with *belly boxes* (storage compartments) and *balloons* (pneumatic tyres). The late Arthur Fenwick and Mrs. Rich are pictured in the foreground

(above right) Stanley Thurston's 'Atomic Thriller' loads leaving Northampton Midsummer Meadow—late 1950s

(below left) Walter Hoadley's living van

(below right) The build-up at Nottingham Goose Fair—late 1950s—a motley collection of vehicles

pletion or propped up on trestles for repair. In the 1920's William Wilson, a prominent *riding master*, travelled an average of 6,000 miles a year. Although he owned a sizeable villa in Peckham he preferred to leave this to his family and spent the winter in his luxurious van—parked in the back yard.

Today the most expensive homes are built in the form of articulated vehicles —this way the length restriction is not so critical. But sensible planning and the quality of warmth remain. Legislation demands a separate Elsan privy, and on many grounds clothes' lines are forbidden. Although the 'showmen's charter' contained in the Public Health Act of 1936 gives protection for the van-dweller, the establishing of winter quarters becomes more difficult each year.

To an impressionable public, the showman's wagons are like a colossal advertisement. The *ad hoc* quality of the road train—its mysterious sheeted

Packing truck for George Irvin & Sons' 'Galloper'—crank rods are stored on top, *horse irons* clipped to the side, *horses* and carved work inside

trucks mounted with engines, the tell-tale bulge of *cheese wheels* and the magnificently lettered box trucks containing frames, *roundings* and *horses*—these are unmistakable indications of pleasures to come. And behind them comes the four-wheeled elegance of the living van, panelled and lined with gold leaf, belly compartments under, and roses painted round the door. To the showman, travelling is an instinct, an inherent quality rooted in antiquity.

New techniques in hydraulics, the diesel tractor and so on, are having very real applications on the fairground. Already the *gun carriage* centre has emerged —in essence a reversion to the Savage centre truck—and rides are becoming more and more compact. The availability of war-surplus heavy tractors in the late 1940's gave the road-train a new look. Such vehicles have proved of particular value to showmen as they are capable of drawing heavy loads and doing double duty generating electric power. The visual importance of the road train is still appreciated by many showmen with their ideas of livery and brand image—but slowly and surely a new transport aesthetic is emerging.

(opposite page top) Unloading the *swifts* of the 'Looper', Mitcham Fair 1966

(bottom) Traction unit for Charles Thurston's 'Swirl', Oxford St. Giles Fair 1966

A dust cart mechanism ingeniously adapted serves to lift the 'Paratrooper' centre Mitcham Fair 1966

swifts and centre assembly loaded— Harvey's 'Juvenile Autodrome' Mitcham Fair 1966

THE CHANGING IDIOM

The steam engine was one thing, but electricity and the internal combustion engine were quite another. The joy ride effervesced with speed, ozone, and dirigible cars. When showman John Walter Waddington replaced his *gondolas* with faithful copies of his own De Dion motor car a sedate period ended. The progression through racing cars to aeroplanes and jet planes was breathtaking, and more than a little bumpy.

The motor-car craze affected not only the 'Scenic' but 'Gallopers' too. After 20 years or so, the novelty of the *horses* began to wear a bit thin, and gradually they were discarded. In their place *motor-cars*, and, immediately after the First World War, even miniature tanks were fitted. The adaptation involved was both uncomfortable and visually unsatisfactory, and in a disastrous period some of the finest sets of 'Gallopers'—stripped of their *horses* and *cockerels*, the *top motion* obsolete, the *spinning frame* too slow and unexciting to simulate a ride in a motor-car—were inevitably scrapped. Hills and valleys in the switchback, and spectacular scenery with electric lighting, were altogether a more suitable medium.

But in time the discipline of a circular track, notwithstanding its undulations, proved tedious and not really expressive of the freedom of movement possible in a motor-car. Characteristically, the whims of the riders reverted to the romanticism of phantom figures like dragons, dolphins and whales. The

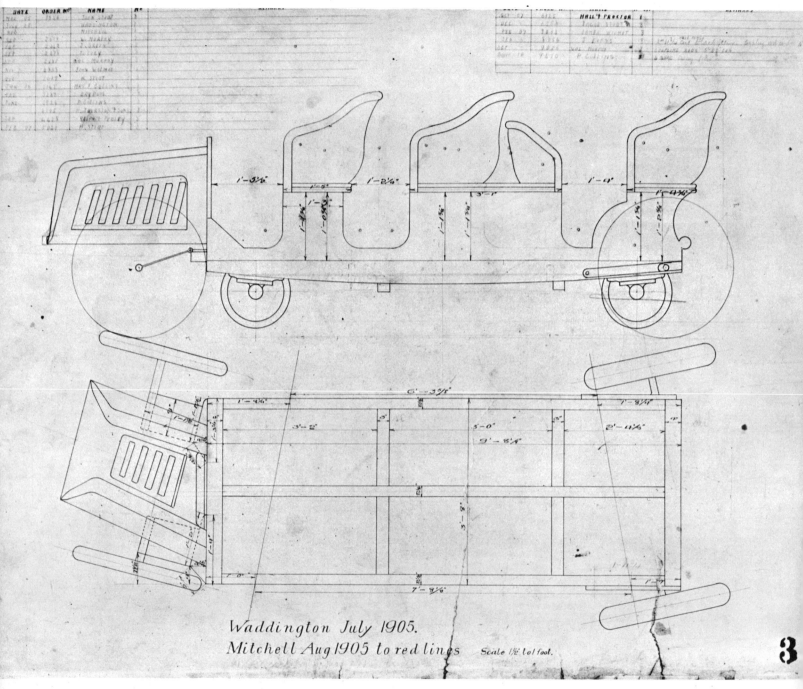

Waddington July 1905.
Mitchell Aug 1905 to red lines   Scale 1½: to 1 foot.

3

Detail of J. W. Waddington's switchback *motor-car*—a design of considerable ingenuity based on this showman's own De Dion

(above right) The head of a 'Scenic Dragon' —typical of the wood carver's art at this time

(right) A children's roundabout with dummy motor-car substituted for *horses*

100

wood carvers at Burton-upon-Trent (Messrs. Orton, Sons & Spoóner) were in their element again, and magnificent gilded monsters began to appear. It was left to Americans, Riehl and the Lusse Brothers, and to Capitelli, to pioneer an amusement device with dirigible *motor-cars*.

Described in part as follows, Stoehrer's Patent (1921 No. 177395) relates to a primitive form of ' Dodg'em ':—

' An amusement device consisting of a running floor, an electrically charged ceiling structure, a car . . . free to travel around the running floor in any direction, a manually shift-able motor-driven combined guiding and traction unit, and an electrical trolley having a promiscuous travelling engagement with the charged ceiling.'

A succession of inventions followed, some of them unnecessarily complicated involving gear change levers, until in 1927 Joseph and Robert Lusse of

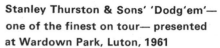

Stanley Thurston & Sons' 'Dodg'em'—
one of the finest on tour— presented
at Wardown Park, Luton, 1961

Italian styling by Spaggiari & Barbieri—
a design reputed to be based on the
Fiat **1300**

The *art nouveau* 'Dodg'em' car produced
by Supercar in the 1930s

Philadelphia produced a very accomplished design. Since that time, 'Dodg'ems' have been the most consistently popular ride on the fairground. As soon as the mechanics were assured the bodywork came in for treatment, and microcosmic motor-car styles evolved.

Portable 'Dodg'em' tracks followed a pattern of standardisation. Initially they were timber framed, but later aluminium was used. They measured 80 ft by 40 ft or 60 ft by 40 ft and were generally oval in plan form, with striped canvas *tilt* and plain *rounding boards*. The balustrading was mounted on spring-loaded bumper boxes at the perimeter. The construction and decoration are discussed in some detail in Chapter 8.

The considerable success of this machine led to a number of perverse designs, including an aquatic variant in the Viennese 'Water Dodg'em'. Fred Markey of Salisbury Beach, Mass., proposed a car with a moveable image, '. . . .simu-

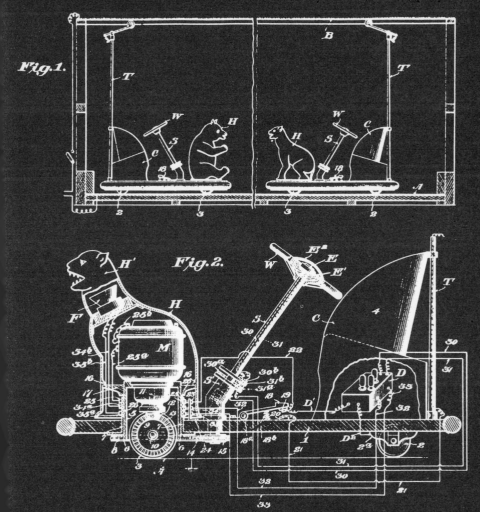

The original patent drawing of Fred Markey's remarkable Dodg'em car, 1932

lating a sound-emitting figure, there being also an occupant's voice amplifying system carried by the car' (extract from the Patent Specification). Thus the driver was enabled to 'broadcast' through the mouthpiece of the image a tirade of abuse to other drivers, much to the delight of spectators. Two years later Markey patented a 'Motor-Cycle Dodg'em'.

Today no fair is complete without its 'Dodg'em' track—Nottingham Goose Fair seldom has less than ten. The spark and scrape of the trolley in essence is a tactile expression of the miracle of electricity. The excitement of driving one's own car, being able to bump or dodge at will, ensures continued success.

The racing car as an amusement device evolved surprisingly early (in 1909), with an invention by Frank and Rolli Fageol of Oakland, California:—'A racing pleasure railway comprising a plurality of tracks, electrically operated cars propelled over said tracks and means for continuously and automatically varying

A 'Monte Carlo Rally' track with miniature racing cars by Supercar

the speed of one car relatively to the other cars during the racing movement thereof . . . (and) wherein steering mechanism is provided for each car for guiding the same in accordance with changes in the line of the track.'

Around 1926 Capitelli invented a track with a steel floor, electrically charged and divided into parallel strips alternately ' positive ' and ' negative '. Miniature racing cars, equipped with a pair of contact brushes, were free to move over the track in more or less parallel paths, certainly with greater freedom than was possible with Fageol's system.

In 1937 Arthur Henry Bland of Wembley, Middlesex, patented the ' Monte Carlo Rally ' or ' Brooklands Speedway ', a refinement of Capitelli's design having an oval-shaped track with centre island and steeply-cambered curves. But with bumping in the ' Dodg'em ' tradition difficult, movement confined to one direction only, and the opportunity to vary one's path fairly limited, the ' Monte Carlo Rally ' has never really caught on.

Just as the aeroplane had many strange antecedents—for example, da Vinci's flying machine, and much later the intrepid bird men—no less obtuse were the early amusement devices simulating flight. In 1888 *gliding swans* were introduced as roundabout cars, and 20 years later Joseph Thewlis, a sculptor from Leeds, designed an immense ' Flying Bird ' roundabout. Each *bird* seated ten and had wings which were made to flap either automatically or by a lever operated by one of the riders. With *swifts* rotating over an undulating track, and the *birds* suspended from them, Thewlis's machine anticipated somewhat the ' Mont Blanc ' or ' Airways ' introduced in the early 1930's.

Airships suspended on chains from a *spinning frame*, and free to swing out as the machine accelerated, were introduced around 1904. After the First World War ' Flying Chairoplanes ', utilising the same principle, were imported from Germany. With the German Mark devalued a set of ' Chairs ', complete with Brüder organ, cost about £500. Many of these are still operating today, whereas the ' Mont Blanc ' or ' Airways ' referred to earlier has, in the last 20 years, disappeared from the fairground completely.

An invention of rather less consequence was the ' Dive Bomber ' by Lee Ulric Eyerly of Salem, Oregon, *c.* 1938. Two revolving cabins were pivoted at the ends of independently-rotating arms. Capable of either looping the loop or being checked mid flight and suddenly reversed, the ride was nothing if not exciting. But with a maximum of eight paying passengers, and a complexity of highly stressed moving parts, profitable operation was difficult to achieve.

' Flying Jets ' are an innovation of the 1950's, with ' Hurricane Jets ' and ' Vampire Jets ' as variants. Built up from a centre truck, the circular motion is imparted by an electric motor. Individual cars have a joy stick to control their elevation, and this action is achieved by means of compressed air. In Italy

Hoadley's 'Mont Blanc'

A German-built 'Flying Machine'—
elaborate predecessor of the better
known and more profitable 'Chair-o-
Plane'

Savage's 'Womp'—forerunner of the
modern 'Swirl'. Reuben Brett, designer
of the machine, is shown in the centre
with Adam Brown, Works Manager, right,
and John Stephenson Pilling, left.

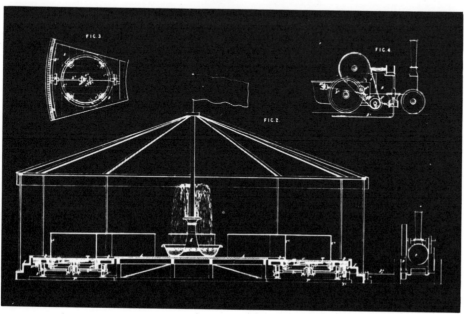

Percival Everitt and Charles Burrell's
'Waltzing Machine'.
Both Everitt and Burrell were prolific
innovators in the sphere of agricultural
machinery

a ' Jet ' machine has been produced where passengers can shoot down the plane in front!

It was reasonable enough that sooner or later compounded movement, the complexity of wheels within wheels, should be exploited by the roundabout builders. In 1914 German-born William F. Mangels, then working in Brooklyn, New York, invented the ' Whip '. Six tub-shaped cars, connected to a continuous revolving chain, were drawn round an oval-shaped track. Each car, being pivoted, swung out on negotiating the semi-circular ends of the track, and this sudden release, an arc within the greater arc described by the whole machine, probably inspired the name. One or two American-style ' Whips ' are still on tour in this country. In the 1920's Savages of King's Lynn produced a ride known as the ' Womp '. This was a variant of the ' Whip '. The track was circular, and a *spider frame* drew eight four-seater cars. Pedal release was incorporated to allow the cars to pivot more or less freely and at the will of the riders. Re-named the ' Swirl ' by showmen, this ride was considerably refined by Thurston, Thurston and Lakin's Patents of 1929 and became one of the fastest rides on the fairground.

Around 1881 Percival Everitt and Charles Burrell designed a charming roundabout which was, alas, never built. The basic idea, however, was most important as it considerably influenced later rides. A traction engine drove the outer ring, and circular platforms were mounted above the main axles, bevel gears and a pair of clutches enabling them to be rotated clockwise or anti-clockwise once the ring was in motion. In the words of the original specification ' . . . the several disc platforms may, if desired, receive an independent rotary motion, and thus groups of persons carried by the several platforms will appear to spectators to mingle after the manner of waltzers . . . the pleasurable sensation of whirling round being at the same time real and to some extent inspiriting, the strains of the organ being timed to suit the progress of the waltzers, and the splash of the fountains being kept up during the dance.' Here, for the first time, were music and movement closely interrelated in a pleasure machine. Although the ' Cakewalk ' approached this, the relationship was not as subtle. In 1920 H. P. Jackson's roundabout with waltzing discs moved a stage further, and ten years later the ' Waltzer ' as we know it today emerged. A *spinning frame* driven round an undulating track carried segmental platforms, and on each platform, freely pivoted, was a *waltzer* car. The resultant movement compounded circular, undulating and tilting motions. In 1933 Lakin and Thurston patented certain improvements, and in the same year one of the first ' Waltzers ' was supplied to the Thurston family.

In the same period *dragons, dolphins and whales*, these ponderous gilded figures, eventually gave place to smaller *one-* and *two-seaters* in a further

rationalisation of the switchback. The transition from *top motion* to 'Scenic' has already been traced. Now, with a single powerful electric motor at the centre, the *swifts* of the *spinning frame* became axles running over a one-rail undulating track. Platforms, hinged between them, formed a convenient basis for *animals* of any description, for *chariots, motor-cycles* or what-have-you. Even conversion to a 'Waltzer' was a simple matter. The collective name 'Noah's Ark' was given to this new ride—a far cry indeed from sedate *platform gallopers* known as the 'Steam Circus'. Centre scenery gave place to a pay box decorated with some restraint, and the organ, in a majority of cases, was super-seded by the *panatrope*, a record-player with powerful amplifier. Gramophone records were a good deal cheaper than cardboard music, being more easily mass-produced, and they could therefore be regarded as expendable. The life of a pop tune had become much shorter.

The invention of the 'Noah's Ark' is attributed by some authorities to the Germans, but it has its roots in the 'Mountain Ponies', a ride created by show-man George Green in the late 1880's. Here *three-abreast horses* were mounted on segmental platforms and driven round an undulating track of two hills and two valleys. It is possible that the first 'Arks' were imported, but by the early 1930's Orton, Sons & Spooner of Burton-upon-Trent and R. J. Lakin of Streatham were building them in some quantity. The standard pattern now had three hills and three valleys in a circle approximately 40 ft in diameter with *rounding boards*, balustrading, bottom shutters and steps.

Still among the *animals*, the 'Caterpillar' made its first appearance in the early 1920's. Carriages, which at the start of a switchback ride were open, became shrouded with a green canvas hood once the machine had gained momentum. The appearance of this snake-like train certainly merited the name. The 'Octopus', on the other hand, had almost no affinity with the eight-footed aquatic. A revolving *spider-frame*, with cars freely pivoted at the end of each arm, was made to revolve about a doubly-eccentric axis.

Mechanical 'Gallopers' and the regal plungings of the *gondola* no longer satis-fied. The roundabout idiom had been transmuted by the age of speed, by science fiction, and all to the accompaniment of pop and jazz. The quest for thrills and excitement led to much faster rides, and carved opulence gave place to naive interpretations of the modern movement and to symbols of outer space. The elemental spoked wheel, ablaze with lights, began to emerge from the labyrinth of sleepers and trestles, tiresome trappings of the portable switchback. The 'Moon Rocket' pioneered a new concept in pleasure riding and the 'Satellite' followed. With dance movements evoked by the 'Twist', and aerial excitement provided by the 'Paratrooper', one can only wait, in breathless astonishment, for the next expression of joy.

A Civic Opening of Kings Lynn Mart in the 1920s—the open top 'Caterpillar' shown on the left was then a brand new concept in riding devices

CONSTRUCTION AND DECORATION 1

The architecture of the fairground did not evolve, and is not contrived. Masquerading as Baroque, Rococo, Byzantine, it is the perfect lampoon of ponderous and weighty styles. It was first informal, then gaudy, ostentatious, opulent—the visions of the working man externalised—an extravaganza of pop idioms, concentrated, mirrored and glittering accompanied by noisy pop music. It has always been so. Transcending the dreary confines of industrial erosion—miles of terraced housing interspersed with bleak, blind factories—the fair created an atmosphere wholly unique, powerful, self-contained, a blaze of light and colour. Freed from imposed academicism and the stuffy eclecticism of the schools, constructions and decorations enjoyed a vitality all their own, geared as they were to amusement, exhilaration and delight. The only disciplines were those that derived from the technique of demountability and reduction to road trains.

The raw materials were simple enough—red deal for framing, best quality pine for carved decoration, clever ironmongery for jointing, striped canvas awnings and some pretty spirited painting. There were no architects, except perhaps the showmen themselves, and the names of designers, sculptors and scenic artists have, for the most part, been forgotten. The following extracts from Savage's order book, dated March 1922, are perhaps typical of the kind of brief given to roundabout builders. They illustrate the considerable influence

Fairground Architecture

Leon Steppe's switchback built-up at Savage's Works prior to despatch—February, 1923

Cross-sectional drawing of Steppe's switchback showing centre engine, *cradle* or *cheese* wheel and *spinning frame*—notice the 3-rail track and implied rolling motion to individual *gondolas*

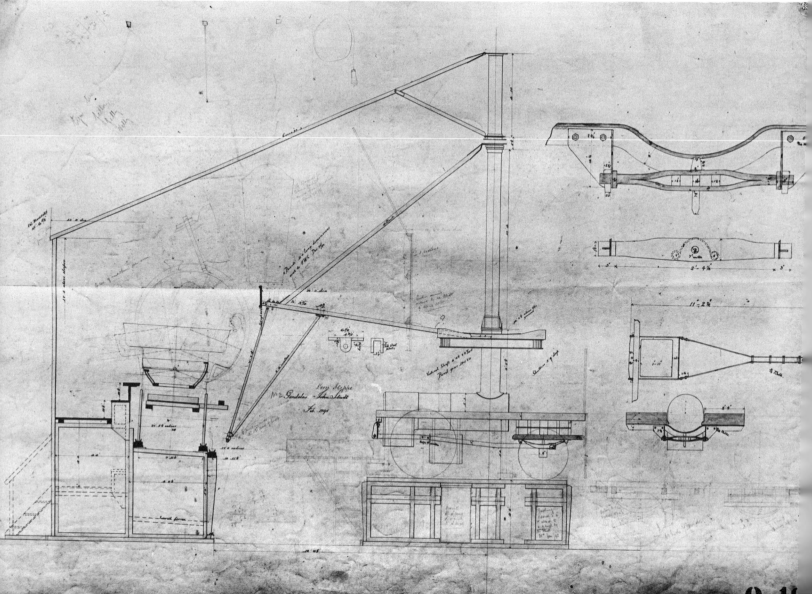

of the showman as client and sometimes sponsor—within certain basic parameters the choice of decoration was entirely his. The order was for a new
switchback to replace Leon Steppe's original machine which had been
destroyed by fire, near Calais, at the time of the armistice in 1918. Eye-witness
accounts suggest that this was the finest switchback ever built at King's Lynn.
The extracts are verbatim:—

' A new switchback railway consisting of all necessary framing, gates, sleepers
and 3 tramways. Handrailing fitted round framing. Run-ups at the bottom of
the hills back and front. Gates to be made in one piece to include ' V ' frames.
Shutters fitted round the framing outside to be lettered:
Proprietaire   Leon Steppe
The first word to be in small letters and the name in large letters. Posts 17′ 0″

Centre assembly and *spinning frame* stripped of decoration—notice the complex pattern of sleepers and *gates* to carry the undulating track and platform—Steppe's switchback

***Gondolas*, shutters and handrails, and scenic *rounding boards* in position—Steppe's switchback**

high, above the sleepers. Fixed top 53′ 2″ dia. Inside wallings to be of red and white canvas to fix against the inside of the switchback gates. Pulling rods for the top framing to be cased with twisted brass. . . . Upright posts to be plain as he (Leon Steppe) is going to fit figures at a later date. Handrails to be fixed with balustrading.'

The order book continues as follows:—

' 8 Gondola cars. Gilded and carved. (In Louis XV style), with brass handrails, upholstered in crimson plush. With cotton covers and green waterproof covers. Concave mirror in back seat and small glass each side of hood, 3″ axles, wheels solid cast iron, brass bushed.
8 pulling rods between the cars with universal ring couplings, and cased with 4 twist brass, with mounts for same.
8 sets of safety canvases between the cars, with chains and stretchers.
Inside and outside footboards to the cars.
A set of carved and gilded top centre with drum and droppers.
Glasses in the droppers only. Carved in the Louis XV style.
A new outside carved garter with glasses.
A carved and gilded pay-box with side widows to open in the same way that railway carriage windows open. Carved in Louis XV style.
A new set of carved and gilded rounding boards. Carved Louis XV style. Boards 43″ deep. With top cornice and droppers, with small fantastic figures at the top of each post appearing to support the boards.
8 small carriages for transporting the Gondolas along the road. These carriages to be arranged with axle and 2 wheels . . . with suitable pulling arrangements.
3 covered trucks 21′ 0″ long, with rounded roofs and with shafts.
2 flat top trucks with shafts, and with 5 uprights on each side and green cover to each also iron bows for the top for the covers to lie on. These wagons to be 21′ 0″ long. The width and height to be made to suit your railway gauges.'

The basic form of the machine was then drawn up by Savage's own designers and full-size templates made of panels to be carved. Working from these, the appropriate style of decoration, in this case Louis XV, was imposed. Artists in France and Italy were often commissioned to do this, and at one time Savage's opened a workshop at 26 Cross Street, Islington, where Italian craftsmen were specially employed. With alternative designs drawn on the reverse side the templates were returned to King's Lynn for the carvers to work from. For Steppe's switchback 12 carvers, who came from London and Birmingham, worked with Albert Arthur Bailey, Savage's regular carver, who later became foreman for the job. Charles Mumford, of W. Sconce & Sons, Scenic Artists, Lynn, painted and lettered the rounding boards, and real gold leaf was applied by R. and B. Frost (father and son), gilders who were employed full time by

(left) Bottom shutters in position and the
spinning frame taking shape with *swifts*,
quarterings and rafters—Ashley's
'Galloper'

Centre truck on trams, organ truck
(sheeted) and packing truck to the rear
—Ashley's 'Galloper'

Savage's. The order, which included repairs to the centre engine salvaged from the fire of 1918, took 11 months to complete, and cost in the region of £9,000.

Steppe's switchback, resplendent in white and gold, went to the Wembley Exhibition where for three months it was operated by showman Patrick Collins. Leon Steppe became ill, and Mme. Steppe came to Lynn to complete the purchase. By the time the machine had reached France, Leon Steppe had died. Very soon after, it was again destroyed by fire.

In the diversity of roundabout types already discussed, a unifying pattern existed. The elements of centre assembly, *spinning frame* and suspended platform, or bottom frame, were common denominators. As structural grids and cross-section generators they dictated the basic form; elevations and interiors, depending on applied decoration, were, as we have demonstrated, to the showman's own whim. In order to amplify this point, and to illustrate the disciplines imposed by demountability, the construction of a 'Galloping Horse' roundabout is worth describing in some detail. Components can be analysed and the sequence of building-up established. Although one machine has here been selected, reference will later be made to frame variants and to alternative types of decoration.

By no means a thoroughbred, W. H. & E. Ashley's roundabout is perhaps more typical because of the impromptu nature of its make-up. Unique among all others, it is the only set of 'Gallopers' to have retained steam-drive to this day. Built in the 1890's by Thos. Walker of Tewkesbury, with a Tidman *centre* and *top motion*, the Savage centre engine was not installed until 1946. New hand-carved horses, by Orton, Sons & Spooner, were fitted in 1925, but two of the original cockerels by Anderson of Bristol have been retained. The organ, a rare Gavioli barrel organ, was taken from a 'Cakewalk'.

The centre truck and engine is blocked up on trams. The chimney, which is also the upper part of the centre pole, is hinged down in the travelling position. The cruciform hub which takes the weight off the road wheels has stays from each corner to the centre pole, one arm passing between the axles. The centre drum is divided into 14 flat faces, 13 of which are mirrored, the 14th acting as an access panel. Two copper bands at the top of the drum, and two fixed metal brushes, conduct electric current for lights in the *spinning frame*. Above the centre drum is mounted the *cheese* wheel with open steel bands into which are slotted the *swifts*. Like the drum, the *cheese* is also divided into 14 sections, giving 14 rows of horses, arranged, in this case, *three-abreast*. Top gearing, which imparts the galloping motion through cranks, is fixed above the *cheese*.

Levelling the trams and winching the centre truck on to them—a removable ramp is provided—is the first part of the operation. When blocked and bolted in position the hub is stabilised. Working platforms around the drum hinged to the truck are lowered and propped from the trams. The organ truck is manœuvred into position and the packing truck brought alongside to provide a working platform for assembling the *spinning frame*. Paybox and bottom shutters, enclosing both trucks and concealing the underworks, complete the centre assembly.

The chimney is then fixed in a vertical position as an extension of the centre pole. The *swifts* are slotted and pinned, and the *quarterings* fastened. The *swifts* are tilted upwards slightly and the ends are tied by steel rods to the centre pole. These ties, which also act as rafters for the canvas awning, can be tensioned by a turn-buckle when the frame is loaded. The crank rods, which rest in bushings placed centrally on the *quarterings*, are then locked in position and engaged with the *top motion* gearing. With the canvas *tilt* secured a large umbrella is formed and the remainder of the building-up can be done under cover. Because the *roundings* can be the most distinctive feature great care is normally lavished upon them. Often they are the most ornate part of the machine, and where lettering is used the choice of words, and of lush type-face, is of prime importance. Ashley's Roundabout is no exception:—
' Ashley's — Grand — Stud of — Electric — Jumping — Horses — Safety & — Pleasure — Combined — Patronised — by the — Elite — of the — Country '.

' Electric ' here refers to the mode of lighting, and not to the drive. *Roundings* are made up of three parts—first the *rounding board* fixed vertically at the

Rounding boards, domes and droppers—
an emphatic capping— Ashley's 'Galloper'

end of the *swifts*, curved in plan form—then the *domes*, mounted above the board, either vertically or tilting forward as with Ashley's—finally the *droppers* which hang below the rounding board and are usually scalloped in profile.

Horse rods, sheathed in twisted brass, are then suspended from the cranks and the *horses* and *cockerels* keyed into position. At the same time the *top centre* shutters are fixed, together with a further set of *droppers*. Platform rods, diagonally braced on the inner ring, the platform segments—14 of them—and double steps complete the main assembly. Banners are hung from the *swifts*, and electric lamps, tightly spaced, festoon both underside of *spinning frame* and top side of *rounding boards*. Thus a three-load road train is transformed into a 'mass of gold and glitter' (an expression coined by American 'Carousel' builder C. W. Parlker)—38 ft in diameter and with *horses* jumping $2\frac{1}{2}$ cycles per revolution.

Top centre and organ front—Ashley's 'Galloper'

The bottom shutters are incised with scroll work, a classical motif freely adapted with bizarre consequences. The admixture of diamond-shaped mirrors and a garland of lettering add to the confusion. The central feature, an ellipse, is obscured by the paybox. On the return end the motif is repeated, but in this case painted on to a flat surface and to a different scale. The pay box is a good deal restrained by comparison; it has cylindrical shafts, a curved and deep scalloped canopy, and a marble-textured base. Ranged behind this is an inner ring of shutters crowned with gilded foliage and cut glass mirrors. The engine shutter bears the owner's name in the top segment, has a gilded edge moulding emphasised by electric lamps, and panels that are flat-decorated with a further variant of the scroll—clearly a quarter stencil used eight times over—giving an effect of doily-like nicety.

The *top centre*, again incised carving, is of unusual design and has an almost primitive quality. In each of the panels the central emblem depicts a rider and prancing horse. An arbitrary arrangement of vegetable-like foliage and diamond-etched panels fills the remainder of the space, and each of the 14 *droppers* has a central shield enclosed by scrolls. Both *swifts* and *quarterings* were originally delicately lined and stencilled. The organ front has been much debased, but the dragon motif, three exquisite figures, and a fine range of brass trumpets remain.

The *horses*, powerfully posed, are painted in vivid colours. Many are individually named after famous racehorses, and the decoration is of extraordinary vitality, varying from mount to mount. Both bridle and mane are carved with meticulous care. The total concept is reminiscent of the spectacular over-dressing of the mediæval 'Carousel', which is perhaps the strong thread of development consciously or unconsciously applied.

The *roundings* with forward sloping *domes* have a fine dynamic quality. Strong cornices to the boards, and the alternation of carved motif with flat areas of lettering, accentuate this quality, while the scalloped droppers, and lights on the underside of the spinning frame, create a busy stroboscopic effect when the machine is in motion. The *domes* are flat-painted with an edge moulding, and shells, scroll-work and a grotesque head combine to form the carved element arranged at the joints between boards. The lettering, contained within piped panels, has a splendid three-dimensional quality and is perhaps the finest example in the country. 'Barley sugar' brasswork encases the platform rods too, and the platform itself is painted to the outline of a 14-pointed star, with the back of the steps striped vertically.

Notwithstanding common denominators, the performance of the *spinning frame*—horizontal, undulating or compounded movement—and the actual

Bottom shutter and pay box—Ashley's 'Galloper'
(bottom) Centre engine and engine shutter —Ashley's 'Galloper'

provision for riders, in cars, in *chariots* or on the backs of *animals*, were the real trend setters. Theme and motif were suggested by the character of the ride, and the progress from *horses* to more sophisticated means of transport saw a remarkable transformation not only in the form of construction, but in the mode of decoration, too.

The ' Galloping Horse ' roundabout, and for that matter ' Dobbies ' too, were unique in that the whole machine was suspended about the centre pole; the only elements that required to be accurately set out and levelled were the centre truck and organ truck. Literally everything else hung from the *spinning frame*. Not so the switchback, where undulating tracks were carried by trestles of varying height. These, in turn, were supported on radial sleepers, each one of which had to be separately levelled, and further complications arose out of the precise plan-form which was not circular but elliptical. Because of the

A carved *gondola* illustrated in Savage Brothers' 1902 Catalogue

A *fixed top* electric 'Motor Car Scenic' with deep *roundings* and centre scenery —see also Chapter 8

height of the hills relative to ground level, both spinning frame and centre engine had to be raised until the boiler was at least 7 ft above the ground.

Spinning top and *fixed top* switchbacks had a platform for spectators following the profile of the track and usually cantilevered from the trestles; the platform, of course, involved steps or ramp, a further item to be set out and levelled. In the *fixed top* variety, spectators were protected from the elements as *tilt* and rafters extended over to fixed uprights at the circumference. There was a further benefit in that roundings could be made much deeper without adding weight to the *spinning frame*.

It is obvious, therefore, that building-up operations for the switchback involved considerable skill and occupied a good deal of time. A *horse* could be fairly easily man-handled, but a richly carved *gondola* with heavy underworks required either a special gantry or an engine crane to lift it on to the track.

But because loads were more evenly distributed—from track, via trestles, to the sleepers, as opposed to the 'Galloper' where almost the full load was concentrated on the cruciform hub—the switchback could be made a larger and heavier machine. Compared with a modest 36 ft to 38 ft in diameter and 14 ft from steps to top of *roundings* in the 'Galloper', switchbacks were often more than 50 ft in diameter, 17 ft to the rafters, and 28 ft to the apex.

Both 'Galloper' and switchback had a fixed centre, but whereas in the 'Galloper' everything else revolved, the switchback was essentially a static enclosure the form of which was dictated by an elevated *spinning frame* drawing *cars* round an undulating track. It is an important distinction, for the *spinning frame expressed*, or the *spinning frame contained*, led to quite different treatment in terms of decoration.

The conversion of switchbacks to electric drive around 1910 made both

Hoadley's 'Motor-Cycle Speedway'—a strictly functional centre assembly with painted *roundings*

Mr Billy Ashley's Three-abreast 'Galloping Horses'

The original frame built by Thomas Walker of Tewkesbury,
Gloucestershire c. 1895

DRAWN BY DAVID BRAITHWAITE

engine and *spinning frame* obsolete and liberated a good deal of space at the centre, soon to be filled with scenery. Great emphasis was then thrown on decoration, both within and without, and special mechanical and lighting effects abounded. Large organs, salvaged from the ' Bioscope Shows' discussed earlier, formed useful centre-pieces too. The expanded surface area of the deeper roundings was treated very much in a romantic idiom, reflecting at first the spirit of adventure implied by the motor-car, and later, perhaps in retrospective attitude, the unspoiled sublimity of under-water scenes. Father Neptune and his entourage were clearly more in keeping with the *dolphins* and *whales* that replaced the *motor-cars*.

In structural form there was little difference between the ' Scenic' and the earlier switchback. It was, after all, only a conversion job, and most of the work involved was in re-modelling the centre. The *cars* and resultant decoration merely reflected current fashionable trends. But the impact of faster, light-weight machines was considerable, and led to a significant rationalisation of structural elements.

'The Autodrome', a product of the 1930's, was compact and offered a really fast ride. Substantially stripped of ornamentation, with flat roundings, some chromium plate and a very stark centre, it contrasted strikingly with the bucolic flavour of John Collins' ' Motor-Car Scenic Railway' of about 1913. The latter had tree trunk uprights, a log cabin pay-box, rustic handrails, and a waterfall! Like the ' Autodrome', the ' Noah's Ark' had steel *swifts*, which were also axles, radiating from a *cheese* wheel mounted only a few feet above ground level. In the case of the ' Ark' a two-wheel or four-wheel centre truck came into use, with the *spinning frame* powered by a single electric motor.

Both of these rides, and the ' Waltzer' and ' Caterpillar' too, retained an undulating track, platform and steps, fixed rafters and roundings, but the form was altogether more austere than the ' Scenic'. Decoration veered away from the Baroque and Rococo and the romantic Pre-Raphaelite, to the highly-varnished realism of speed images. The organ and scenery had now vanished, leaving only a flat-painted pay-box with celluloid windows.

The ' Dodg'ems' and ' Monte Carlo Rally' involved enclosed arenas for free-moving cars. As such, they comprised a steel floor built on sleepers, peripheral uprights, and trussed and raftered roof. The ' Dodg'ems' included an electrically charged wire net ceiling, and the ' Monte Carlo Rally' a centre island. In a sense the ' Swirl', too, was an arena for compounded motion of the *spider frame* and its freely-pivoted cars. In each case the vitality came from the design of the cars, and only to a lesser degree from the applied decoration of *roundings* and balustrading.

The 'Autodrome'—speed and chromium plate

Murphy's 'Chair-o-Plane' in the Tyneside area

But in the case of ' Chair-o-planes ', ' Jets ' and the ' Octopus ' the *spinning frames* are expressed. In the former, high suspension points for the chains and a raised platform for the riders to mount ensure that the chairs swing out clear of the heads of spectators. With drum and *top centre* divided into segments the opportunity for lining and scenic painting is used to the full. The revolving truncated cone is the powerful element, however, particularly when seen at night with the emphasis of rows of electric lamps. ' Jets ' and ' Octopus', in visual terms the unabashed expression of the elemental spoked wheel, rely wholly on lamps and on the machine aesthetic of a complex hub. Both are built up from a central fulcrum and there are no sleepers or rafters. Speed, and in the case of the ' Octopus ' an eccentric motion, are the basis of their popular appeal.

CONSTRUCTION AND DECORATION 2

It would be difficult to establish a sequence of styles in fairground architecture
much as one had the Orders of Architecture. It is true that pattern books of
the French Renaissance gave a degree of assurance and, for a time at least, a
positive sense of direction. But beyond this, the real design objectives were
lost in the enigma of folk-lore. *Roundings* and shutters were like so much
empty canvas waiting to be sensitised by the visions of the simple man. Only
the basic forms were constants, generated as they were by pure mechanics.

In the broad terms of development so far outlined these constants, or common denominators, are here set out and the modes of decoration evaluated on
a strictly comparative basis. Some attempt has been made to arrange them
chronologically, but inevitably the periods can only be loosely defined.

The centre assembly and spinning frame
From earliest beginnings the hub, or *cheese*, of the *spinning frame* has been
mounted on a vertical axle. Starting with a wooden spoked wheel, like a great
cartwheel on a wooden post, advancing designs had the rim stabilised by tie
rods and the axle seated in a cross formed by two baulks of timber. Suspended
horses and carriages involved a higher mounting for the *spinning frame*, and
this in turn necessitated stays from the cruciform hub to prop the taller centre

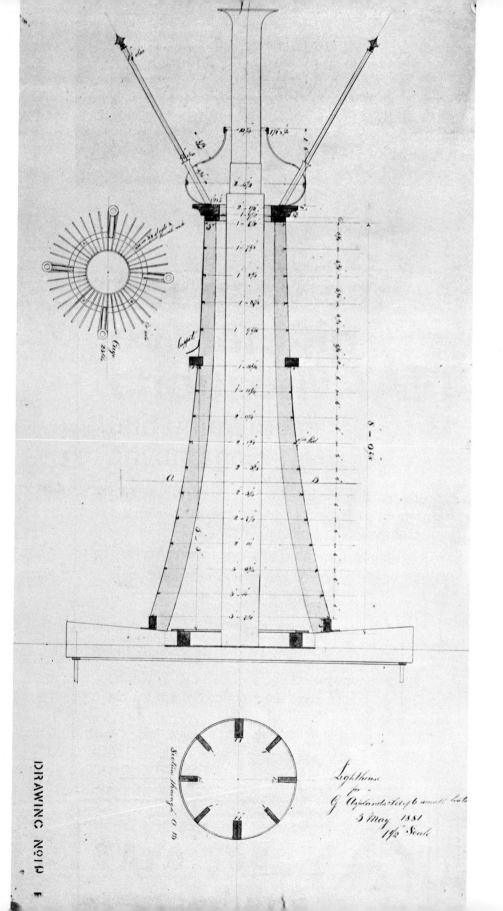

Detail of the lighthouse centre to George Aspland's 'Sea-on-Land' machine—the chimney passes through the middle—see also page 42

pole. As soon as power drive was introduced both engine and gearing had to be dressed up or concealed, and for this purpose decorated shutters were invented. More than this, the chimney, carrying smoke and exhaust steam away from the engine, acted as an extension of the centre pole. Obviously its function could not be ignored, although some attempts were made to disguise it as a lighthouse.

Before mechanical organs came into general use some of the larger round-abouts had a musician's gallery, and this, too, was built up round the centre pole and crowned with a multi-coloured beacon. But when the *spinning frame* became like a giant umbrella an inverted cone of shutters masked the *cheese* and the *top motion* gearing that made the horses gallop. This cone became known as the *top centre*, and it was here that rich carving and cut glass mirrors were concentrated. Below it, the centre drum concealing the drive shaft was

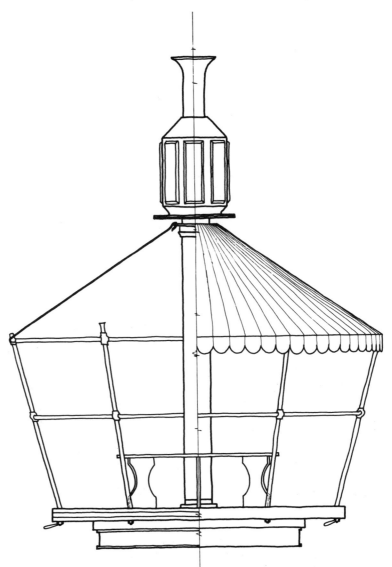

Detail of a Musician's Gallery built by Savages in 1880 for showmen Sanger and Davis—probably for installation in a 'Platform Galloper' or 'Sea-on-Land'. The drawing is based on a Works original now much faded

129

Centre assembly of Percy Cole's (formerly Aspland's) 'Venetian Gondolas' —engine mounted longitudinally, elaborately carved *drum* poised above it

A full-size template for *top centre* shutters drawn in charcoal on stout grey paper—this one has both elliptical and circular panels.

usually mirrored in segments and the individual mirrors framed by *appliqué* carving. Although very much an integral part of the centre assembly the decoration of mechanical organs is dealt with separately under the heading 'Proscenium'.

Concealing the underworks of centre and organ trucks, water tank and other accessories involved a further set of decorated shutters, and very often these, too, were elaborately carved. Sometimes a paybox was incorporated in them.

Elliptical and circular panels in the *top centre* would be filled either with bevel-edged mirrors to reflect the lights, or in the former case with the portrait of a distinguished person. Deriving from the arrangement of engine and truck the centre assembly of the 'Galloper' was pretty much standard, although dimensional variations occurred in the height of the truck depending on whether it had to pass road or railway loading gauge. The diameters of drum and *top centre* varied too, for less functional reasons, but· the elements of applied decoration were always highly individual in design. For this reason no two sets are alike.

Advancing from *horse* to *gondola*, the centre assembly for *top motion* switchbacks differed in the arrangement of the engine, which besides being appreciably larger was mounted longitudinally on the truck. Electric light installations coincided, more or less, with the introduction of the switchback, and the portable light engine—affectionately known as the 'Sparkler'—became a further element in the centre assembly. Existing centre chimneys were cut into and a connecting flue fitted to the light engine.

Further development to the electric-drive 'Scenic', where all heavy machinery was stripped from the centre and the *spinning frame* disappeared altogether, led to the kind of elaboration shown in John Evan's 'Scenic

The Gold Medal Electric
Installation in John
Wilmot's (Glasgow) 'Grand
Steam Driven Cockerel
Roundabout'—a 'Platform
Galloper'

The remarkably ornate centre in John
Evan's 'Scenic Dragons'—in Scotland,
1922

Counter-rotating centre in the 'Moon Rocket'—Walter Shaw's machine at Nottingham Goose Fair, c. 1958

Dragons' of about 1922. Erected at the back of the organ, the fantastic scenery was very much in the idiom of contemporary ' Movie Palaces '. It incorporated a fountain and was brilliantly lit at night. An earlier ' Motor-Car Scenic ' had a waterfall and rustic mill surrounded by fretwork foliage. In striking contrast, the ' Ark ' and ' Waltzer ' that curtailed the gorgeous era of the ' Scenic ' had only a steel pole to carry the paybox and rafters above it.

With an oblique axle and a counter-revolving centre piece, the ' Moon Rocket ' represented a departure from the main stream of development. Rarely seen on fairgrounds today, this heavily-built machine had a circle of *rocket cars* revolving at high speed on an inclined plane. With the centre disc turning in the opposite direction this feeling of speed was much accentuated. In rides like the ' Jets ' and ' Flying Coaster ' the orbit of revolution and the stimulus of speed are all-important. Consequently the centre assembly—again constructed as a truck—is left exposed.

Static Enclosure

The switchback and its descendants—the ' Ark ', ' Autodrome ', ' Waltzer ', ' Caterpillar ', etc.—involve a static enclosure to the *spinning frame*—sleepers, trestles, uprights and rafters. The problems of building up on uneven ground have already been referred to. In all circular rides the sleepers and rafters are set out radially, and the centre pole forms the apex of the canvas *tilt*. Pin joints predominate throughout and bolt fixing is kept to an absolute minimum. Trestles to carry undulating tracks and platforms are fixed to the sleepers and are sometimes propped from the centre. Stays from the centre pole stiffen the rafters and provide support for banners, emblems, and lights. Considered in structural terms, the *roundings*, balustrades and shutters serve as stiffeners between the radial frames. In the case of a ' Dodg'em ' track, wooden sleepers form a rectangular grid. The joists—their length governed by maximum dimensions for packing—usually have staggered joints to give continuity. Diagonal bracing is superfluous as steel floor plates constitute a very solid diaphragm. Substantial wooden uprights carry steel-framed trusses, fabricated in two halves, but intermediate rafters and purlins are again of wood. In the old days a ' Dodg'em ' track weighed all of 40 tons—each floor plate required four strong men to lift it—but now the use of aluminium alloy for framing, and for the plates too, has reduced the load to about 10 tons and the build-up time to only six hours. In France, and perhaps elsewhere, a tubular-framed roof is assembled on the floor of the track and then jacked into position.

The construction of canvas booths relies less on a geometric architectural shape. Wooden posts and scantlings lend only an indefinite form to the billowing mass—carefully-tensioned guy ropes do the rest. But the volume enclosed

(right) Lifting a main truss on the 'Dodg'em'

(far right) A track built by Lang Wheels

(below right) Setting out and levelling the sleepers—A 'Swirl' at Baldock Charter Fair, 1952

(above) Machine aesthetic in the 'Flying Coaster'—J. & H. Shaw's machine at Nottingham Goose Fair, 1963

A four-wheel centre to the 'Waltzer' carrying *cheese* and motor, with pay box cantilevered above

is very often spectacular, as in the case of the circus *big top*—one of the most perfect acoustic shapes. The erection sequence is simple enough—the masts, or *king posts*, are staked out and mechanically winched into the vertical position, and the guy ropes are fixed and tensioned. The sections of canvas are then set out on the ground, about the *king posts*, and laced together with rope. The canvas is attached to collars at the base of the posts, and by means of pulleys these are raised, using either tractor or elephant power. Ring posts and perimeter posts are fixed while the top is being lifted, and each one is guyed.

Notwithstanding the circus tent, the fairground booth pure and simple is usually subordinate to a proscenium. The show front, or the game enclosed, is the essential generator, as typified by the 'Bioscope Shows' and 'Menageries'.

Carriage and Decoration

The decoration of the fairground reflected something of the social changes

The billowing mass of the 'Big Top' is however very vulnerable—(right) the illustration shows the effect of gale-force winds at Newcastle Town Moor Fair in 1927

The proscenium of the famous Bostock & Wombwell Menagerie—notice the musicians on the left of the entrance

A refined jacking system for lifting the top frame of a 'Dodg'em' track in France

Lifting the 'Big Top'—Chipperfield's Circus, late 1940's

taking place. The freedom of expression held by the artist was, in a sense, frighteningly bewildering. Once the lavishness of Baroque had been discarded, the bubble and hiss of a society in ferment were bound to exert strong influences. The progression from *gondola* to *rocket* involved more than structural rationalisation—the carved exuberance of the 19th century gave place to the highly varnished flamboyance of new wrappings.

The impact of the First World War had been shattering, and inevitably there was much searching for new values. Popular images changed radically, and the fluidity of the emergent society veered first towards stubborn romanticism—holding fast to the seeming pleasures of a by-gone age. In industry, the urgency of productivity lapsed, and the whole character of the machine changed from the relentless implement of manufacture to a humanitarian contrivance designed for direct personal benefit. The telephone, the gramophone, bicycle and motor-car, vacuum cleaner and refrigerator, became universally available, and ' talkies ' were soon to be an essential part of life.

The mock elegance and good taste of the Victorian *soirée* gave place to the rumbustious ' Charleston ' and the ' Black Bottom '. Boisterous evenings at the music-hall, where the entertainer's craft dominated, gave place to carnival nights in Ruritania—the cult of musical comedy. The sham opulence of the ' gin palace ' finally gave way to the cold restraint of the road house. The joy ride responded with flashing lights, chromium plate and stupefying speed.

But the relaxed gaiety of the 1920's and the apparent unpreparedness of the 1930's were perhaps deceptive. A new confidence had already emerged and, with new roots secure, the fruits of a new technocratic age were soon to appear.

These were just some of the influences that moved the artist. His untutored expression was crystallised in both ' carriage ' and ' decoration '—his largest medium the rounding board. Because of the high degree of spontaneity, and because of his undisciplined freedom, many of his works must seem like inarticulate mumblings, but the motivations are clear enough.

Originally rounding boards were made from pine and faced with canvas well worked in with white lead before painting. In machines with the *spinning frame* exposed the weight of the *roundings*—and therefore their depth—was usually kept to a minimum. The written statement, arranged in anti-clockwise sequence on the boards, was a better draw than slim panels of scenic painting. Gold leaf was used liberally and a coat of varnish applied to protect the completed unit.

More than just an emphatic capping, *roundings* were in a sense glorious labels, sometimes embodying a much-paraphrased description of the amusement enclosed—to whet the appetite—and sometimes merely evocative. A considerable diversity of types was possible and at the larger fairs contrasting

137

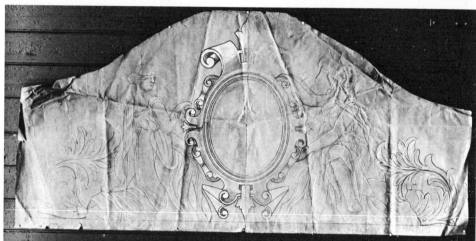

(above) A section of *rounding board* with typical florid lettering whimsically decorated with foliage—notice the triple emphasis of lining, perspective and shadow

(left) Template of a *dome* section

(below left) Alternative designs for *droppers*

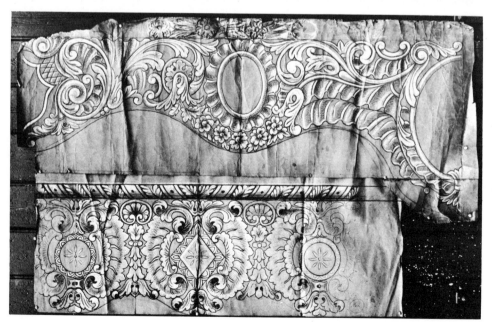

(opposite page) Thomas Walker's No. 11 Machine—a *High Baroque* with luxuriant flowing lines to *domes* and *droppers*, a rich encrustation of mirrors, meticulously painted jungle scenes and an ebullience of flags and bunting

(top right) Screeton Brothers' 'Galloper' (formerly Percy Sheeran's, formerly Joe Brewer's)—ungenerous and spindly lettering, a number of panels in the *domes* are obviously not original, but the complex profile of the *droppers* and the variegated mirrors contained, are most successful

(below) John Barker's *4-abreast* 'Gallopers' has *appliqué* carving to the *domes* and very competently painted battle scenes on the *boards*— notice the arrangement of carved head motif that cleverly masks the join between *boards*

Hull Great Fair in 1908—6 machines built by Savages. From left to right, W. Shipley's *4-abreast* 'Galloping Horses' —a straight *board* with strong cornice, no *domes* or *droppers*; Marshall's 'Motors' has a narrow *board* with high *domes*; Aspland's 'Motors' has a narrow *board* with carved cornice and scalloped *droppers* resting on carved figures; George Green's *4-abreast* 'Giant Bantams' has a unique pagoda-like top, almost certainly the only one ever built; both Waddington's 'Motors' and Patrick Collins' 'Giant Teddy Bears' have deep *roundings* with straight top and scalloped *droppers* (right) A roundabout *centaur*

styles were to be seen in profusion.

The unprecedented elegance of the 'Gondola Switchback' was attributable to a rare coincidence of recognisable Baroque disciplines. Here the decoration of *roundings* with typical Venetian scenes, grotesque figured consoles, and— above all—the fantastic carving of *top centre* and *gondolas*, were all perfectly in balance. Walter Murphy's machine was one of the finest and claimed the unique distinction of being the only switchback ever erected in Madison Square, New York. Decoration appropriate to the motor-car, however, eluded the artists for some years. A 'Motor-Car Scenic', also owned by Walter Murphy, had most accomplished *art nouveau* roundings—much deeper than the earlier example—but neither these nor the incongruous columns and base were in keeping with the new machine aesthetic.

If nothing else, the stubborn romanticism that produced *whales*,

dolphins and *dragons* in reaction to the motor-car ensured a return to consistency in the dream fabric of fairground decoration. John Evan's ' Scenic Dragons ' had an extension front depicting Father Neptune, two rather lush nymphs, and very puckish whales. The *roundings* of John Proctor's ' Peacocks ' were full of fabulous images, painted with considerable verve.

But the delicacy of all these embellishments, glittering Baroque and Rococo too, had little affinity with the new concepts emerging. The images were all wrong, and as soon as the dream was shattered—a brittle and transitory civilisation soon did this—they were just so much icing sugar. Hero-figures of a past era, transmuted by the carvers to roundabout *centaurs*, were suddenly replaced by very plain *waltzing tubs* and the sophistication of a carnival. Even cubism and linear architecture, a notion only partially digested, began to make harsh display on the *roundings*. Everything became short-term—the *panatrope*

141

142

(above) The evocative quality of the *rounding boards*—Barnstable Fair in 1904 (the date on the photograph—1907—is incorrect)

(top left) Walter Murphy's 'Waltzing Gondolas'—one of the finest switchbacks ever built and the only one ever to be erected in New York's Madison Square

(far left) John Proctor's 'Peacock Scenic' at Grantham in the 1920s. The *roundings* were full of fabulous images, and were painted with considerable verve

(left) Carved figure from the organ in Percy Cole's 'Venetian Gondola'

with its three-minute pop tune displaced the mechanical organ—and a nastier opulence was created with simulated marble and chromium plate.

The 'Monte Carlo Rally' and 'Mont Blanc' both had obvious themes for decoration, and speed symbols—straight from the *Boys' Own Annual*—began to grace the front, back and sides of every 'Ark Speedway' in the country. Just as obvious were science fiction symbols for 'Moon Rockets' and dancers for dance movement machines, although the relation between ballet and the 'Waltzer' is perhaps obscure. Unfortunately the bent of the artist was not towards figure drawing, and the result, although not lacking in vigour, was often close to the comic strip. But these were only transitory features in the much expanded tempo of life.

The high varnish of marble texturing, the endless repetition of simple stencilled forms, of wings, circles and ogee's composed in a faintly Byzantine

(left) John Evans' 'Scenic Dragons', 1922
(see also page 134)—the *extension front*
depicted Father Neptune
Walter Murphy's 'Motor-Car Scenic'
had most accomplished *art nouveau*
roundings, much deeper than earlier
examples, but neither these nor the
incongruous columns and base were in
keeping with the new machine aesthetic
(below) Decoration in the 'comic strip'
idiom—Laurence Silcock's 'Waltzer' at
Nottingham Goose Fair, c. 1958
Simulated marble and chromium plate—
Stanley Thurston & Sons' 'Dodg'em' at
Wardown Park, Luton, 1962

manner, relied on crisp definition by electric lamps and on their reflected dazzle. Pine was replaced by plywood, and the whole concept of applied decoration got much thinner in every sense of the word. The importance of individual lighting effects cannot be over-estimated. With gas and naphtha oil as fuel the possibilities were clearly limited; with carbon arc lamps, an intensely powerful spot source, mirrored reflections gave much visual excitement, but with the introduction of individual electric lamps the advantages were manifold. Structural and decorative elements could be emphasised and picked out in different colours, and sections of lamps could be made to flash either in time with the music or at the whim of the *riding master*. The *spinning frame* had long been delineated by electric lamps but, in the final analysis, scarcely anything was left but the machine, the cars, and a mass of lamps.

Irvins' Marenghi organ

'Carnival Nights in Ruritania'— an obvious theme for the 'Waltzer'

Proscenium for a 'Ghost Train' in Finland—the international language of the fairground

Proscenium

The subject of show fronts has already been referred to. The mechanical organ involved a proscenium in microcosm, and no doubt because of the obvious virtuoso skills of organ builders like Gavioli, Marenghi, Hooghuys and others the quality of the artwork was consistent and often highly distinctive. The superb Marenghi organ that accompanies George Irvin and Sons' 'Gallopers' has a flamboyant gilded proscenium incorporating flying horses, dragons, and five beautifully carved automatons. Ranged behind these are the wooden pipes, and at either side the drum stands. By contrast, the Gavioli of Miss Sally Beach has a more restrained and architectural form, with plinth, *pipe colonnade* and Rococo style entablature.

Prosceniums of another sort were used to define entrances to some of the earlier rides. A *spinning top* switchback built by Thomas Walker of Tewkes-

bury had carved and gilded work inset with the usual cut glass mirrors, and two crude caryatids were incorporated. Lighting was by suspended carbon arc lamps. More in the idiom of the 1920's dancing figures were often used to decorate the proscenium of the 'Cakewalk'. The 'Ghost Train', on the other hand, presented an unusual opportunity for painting of evocative quality as illustrated by the fine example from Finland; in the fairgrounds of the world, language is no barrier.

But in general there is little evidence to suggest that show fronts were ever considered as archetypal prosceniums. 'Bioscope Shows' came nearer than any other because of the predominance of an organ front. Whatever vitality there may be comes not from a single artistic concept but more from a series of accidents—the disarray of banners and *gag cards*, the inevitable silver bells, and the parade of performers. A composite design by Gaviolis for a show front in the style of Louis XV embodied a 'Gavioliphone', and suggests what might have been achieved. Described as 'a model of style, artistic carving (with) decorated doors for the entrance and exit of the public', this model was, however, made only upon special request. The organ was extra powerful and represented a 'real orchestra of 120 musicians'.

Proscenium for a travelling show—the centre-piece a mechanical organ—by Gaviolis

High varnish, simple stencilled forms
and reflected dazzle—Stanley Thurston
& Sons' 'Swirl' at Wardown Park,
Luton, 1962

POSTSCRIPT

For centuries the creation of a *tober* has given delight to thousands. The fact that it is so created, and just as quickly dissolved, is part of its essential charm. And as long as there are fairgrounds left the miracle will recur. But take note, planners: each year valuable sites are lost to the so-called developers, and not one of the new towns has a proper *gaff*.

More than half a century ago the sceptics predicted the end of it all, but the total culture of the travelling fair has deep and firm roots. An arduous craft has inevitably bred a tough people—the many exaggerated impresario figures attest this vitality. In fact membership of the Showmen's Guild has doubled in the last 25 years, and so, too, has the number of *rides* on tour. Business isn't what it was and the days are gone when a £20,000 switchback could pay for itself with tuppenny fares, but as yet there is no evidence of a serious decline.

The evanescent mechanical *horses*, gilded *carriages*, *balloons* and *airplanes* are all part of a dream fabric. How sterile by comparison are the *Amusement Park* and the academically contrived *Fun Palace*. The *tober* and its components are conceived intuitively. Some of the pioneer designers were illiterate, but they were all powerfully animated by a common zeal. The realisation of surplus, a product of industrial revolution, gave rise to this zeal and to the need for expressions of joy. The roundabout-builders supplied the need.

The insubstantial architecture of striped awnings, flamboyance and coloured lights, the clamour of *panatropes* and the noxious puff of diesel fumes, the aroma of peas and mint and toffee-apples all-pervading, will continue for many years. The singular colloquialisms of spielers and pitch-getters will merge with the endless cycle of stylus-blunting pop tunes, convoys of balloons will float uncannily above the stalls—until midnight. Then the lights go out, and by daybreak all that is left are patterns in the grass and the deep ruts of massive tyres among discarded fripperies:—

'. . . the baseless fabric of this vision,
The cloud capp'd towers, the gorgeous palaces,
The solemn temples, the great globe itself,
Yea, all which it inherit shall dissolve
And, like this insubstantial pageant faded
Leave not a rack behind. . . .'

The following are some of the terms peculiar to the business of travelling fairs. In many cases everyday words are endued with special meanings, but because of regional differences—showmen being rather introvert in nature—the definitions given will not always be universally correct. In the more detailed historical notes regarding various roundabouts many of the facts have been gathered first-hand from showmen, from retired employees and from innumerable well-informed enthusiasts. Because of the paucity of official records positive authentication is rarely possible. Although human memory is fallible every effort has been made to ensure reasonable accuracy. Many of the details here recorded, and in the biographical section, have not been published before.

Abreast

1-, 2-, 3- and 4-abreast refer to the arrangement, side by side, of *horses*, *cockerels*, *bicycles*, or other vehicles, in a roundabout. Thus '3-abreast Galloping Horses' would have 3 concentric rows of *horses*, and '2-abreast Velocipedes' would have 2 concentric rows of *bicycles*.

Aerial Novelty

see under Razzle Dazzle

Airways

also known as Mont Blanc—a circular ride having a static enclosure, an elevated undulating track and suspended cars. Probably derived from Thewlis' *flying bird* roundabout of 1909. Patents that have some bearing are as follows :—

    1909 – No. 22976 (Thewlis)
    1911 – No. 28099 (Patrick Collins)
    1931 – No. 367670 (Rouge & Sopher)

   The leading builders were Maxwells of Musselborough but in the last 15 years or so the ride has become extinct.

Alpine Slip

also known as Alpine Glide—see under Helter Skelter.

Ark

primarily the collective name for modern switchbacks ; specifically the term 'Noah's Ark' referred to a circular ride having an undulating track—3 hills and 3 valleys, or 2 hills and 2 valleys—and a variety of fixed *animals* carried on segmental platforms, all contained within a static enclosure. The terms 'Ark Speedway', 'Ben

Hur', 'Coronation Speedway', 'Jollity Farm' and 'Motor Cycle Speedway' are roughly synonymous, *animals* being replaced by *chariots* or other vehicles as appropriate. Relevant Patents are as follows:—

    1889 – No. 6140—see also under Mountain Ponies
    1934 – No. 438976 (T. Orton)

Principal builders were Orton, Sons & Spooner of Burton-upon-Trent, and R. J. Lakin of Streatham, London.

Atkins Royal Menagerie *(left)*

a competitor of the great Bostock & Wombwell 'Wild Beast Show'.

As early as 1912 showman Thomas Murphy had his 'Electric Motor-Car Scenic' billed as 'The Autodrome'— then a brand new word, and apparently inspired by Hippodrome.

Banner

specifically an informative notice or slogan, hung from swifts or rafters— sometimes stating the price of the ride, sometimes giving warning on how not to ride.

Belly Irons

part of an alternative suspension for *galloping horses* developed by Tidmans

Atomic Thriller *(above)*

an up-to-date name for the Swirl.

Autodrome

inevitable descendant of the Cyclo-drome, and a rationalisation of the 'Motor-Car Scenic': a circular switch-back with dummy cars mounted on steel swifts that also act as axles, electric motors fitted under some of the cars, and all contained within a static enclosure. A very fast ride, the Autodrome, built primarily by Lang Wheels of Hillingdon Heath (no longer in business), made its debut in the late 1930's.

of Norwich. Instead of the horse iron passing through the body of the *horse* and into a groove in the platform (or into the platform slide), the underside of the *horse* was restrained by these hinged irons fixed to the belly.

Ben Hur

a variant of the Ark having dummy chariots in place of *animals*.

Big Dipper *(facing page)*

a gravity ride having mechanically propelled elevator, or elevators, to haul passenger-carrying cars up the steeper inclines, after which the cars would move under gravity; the big dip gave the initial kinetic energy. Because of the large plan area, the many components required to form trestles, and the immense labour forces required in building-up, Big Dippers were rarely travelled.

Bioscope
literally a motion-picture projector—in terms of the fairground a generic term meaning travelling booth for the display of motion pictures—see also *The Picture Palace and other Buildings for the Movies* by Dennis Sharp in this series.

Boat
the vehicle of a swing, thus a 'Set of Boats' means a set of 'Swing Boats'; also a roundabout car as used in the Sea-on-Land machine, and certain children's roundabouts.

Bottom Centre
refers to the lower half of roundabout centre assemblies, and specifically to decorative shutters enclosing the under-works.

Bowl Slide
a Helter Skelter with a hemi-spherical bowl at the base of the spiral chute.
    1923 – Patent No. 209974 (Wilkie)

Brooklands Speedway
also known as Monte Carlo Rally—an oval shaped *racing track* with electrically-driven miniature racing cars. The following Patents are relevant:—
    1909 – No. 9583 (Fageol)
    1926 – No. 268297 (Capitelli)
    1936 – No. 474947 (Bland)
    1937 – No. 487487 (Bland)
Principal builders were Lang Wheels of Hillingdon Heath and Supercar Co. of Leamington Spa.

Bumper Cars
see under Dodg'em

Burrell Engines and Roundabouts
In partnership with Percival Everitt, Charles Burrell designed the roundabout described on page 107, later registered as Patent No. 5433 (*c.* 1880).
    Patent No. 3423, in 1887, covered the design of a telescopic centre pole.
    A special duo-directional roundabout was built by Burrells around 1890 to the order of The Locomotive Merry-go-Round Co. Ltd.; with a small locomotive drawing carriages in a counter-clockwise direction and 3-abreast 'Gallopers' on the outside revolving clockwise, the machine appears to have been based on a Reynolds & King Patent.
    In 1895 Burrell patented a traction centre with a separate engine mounted on the turret to drive the top cheese wheel, the main engine then being harnessed to a D.C. generator. This invention, although never built, would have solved the problems that arose out of excessive power of the traction centre–1895–Patent No. 21403.
    The last showman's engine built at Thetford was 'Dolphin', No. 4030—it was despatched in September 1925. Even in those days, showmen's engines cost in the region of £1,800.
See also *Chronicles of a Country Works* by Ronald H. Clark.

Cakewalk
originally a dance performed by American Negroes—a prize of a cake was awarded to the most accomplished performer; in terms of the fairground, an amusement device comprising oscillating bridges.
    Relevant Patents are as follows:—
    1902 – No. 11482 (Tilyou)
    1907 – No. 25150 (Taylor, a trailer-mounted unit)
    1909 – No. 3375 (Lawson)
    Orton, Sons & Spooner were principal builders, and Thos. Walker of Tewkesbury produced a similar device known as the 'Dancing Machine'.
    The modest price of £600, for the Walker-built machine, included a waterproof covering.

Wooding's 'Cakewalk' at Cambridge Midsummer Fair, 1958

Calypso *(above)*

a recent open-top machine based on the *wheels within wheels* concept. Clusters of 4 saucer-shaped cars (with protective umbrellas) pivot about the arms of a spider frame which is itself rotating over a gently undulating track.

Carousel or Carrousel

originally an equestrian sport practised in Arabia and Turkey during the 12th century, later an elaborate spectacle involving tournaments, finally a ' Merry-go-Round '. The term Carousel, in this latter sense, is mostly confined to the United States and to the continent.

Caterpillar

a member of the switchback family offering the added excitement of a green canvas hood that enshrouds the cars when they are moving at their fastest. A wind machine, strategically placed under the trestles, gives further delight.

    The following Patents are relevant :—
        1922 – Nos. 197685 and 208505
          (Maynes)
        1949 – No. 667432 (Green)

Centre Truck *(above)*

the heart of the portable roundabout embodying cruciform hub, centre drum, engine and mechanism. In 1900 the cost of a Savage centre truck and spinning frame was £485.

Chair-O-Planes

a high revolving spinning frame with *chairs* suspended on chains. As the frame gathers momentum the *chairs* swing out. A raised platform and steps are provided in order to mount the *chairs*, and many of the earlier models, imported from Germany, had a small mechanical organ. There may have been isolated cases of a steam centre engine.

    Antecedents of the Chair-O-Planes had more elaborate vehicles—miniature air-ships and aeroplanes. The following Patents have some bearing :—
        1888 – No. 13904 (Inshaw)
        1904 – No. 9559 (Barker)

Charter Fair

a fair established by royal charter, as opposed to ancient fairs of Anglo-Saxon and earlier origin which were established by prescription.

Cheese Wheel

the hub of the spinning frame, an open slotted disc into which the spokes, or swifts, are fitted.

Colonial Racing Horse Roundabout

a ' Galloping Horse ' roundabout specially designed and built by Savages of King's Lynn for use in the Colonies. Being a most compact machine, it was distinguished by its abbreviated decorations and general light-weight construction. A number of these machines, including Botton Bros' set, are still in use in this country.

Compensating Rail

specifically the third rail in the Savage-designed switchback bottom. Earlier models, which had a two-rail track, were very prone to derailment problems. In the three-rail system, forward wheels of the *gondola* ran on the outside and Centre Rail and backward wheels on the outside and inside rail, the centre rail compensating against derailment by a subtle variation in the vertical alignment. The following patent is relevant :—
        1888 – No. 15778 (Savage)

Coronation Speedway

usually another name for the Ark, possibly so-called because of its introduction in a Coronation Year and the exploitation of this event in the general decoration and livery.

Cradle Wheel

another name for cheese wheel.

Crane Engine

basically a showman's traction engine having a davit-like jib attached to the rear of the tender for lifting heavy *gondolas* on to their tracks.

Crank *(above)*

specifically that member which imparts galloping motion; in the case of the Platform Galloper a pair of cranks on the main axle of the carrying wheel imparted the motion from underneath; in the case of overhead cranks the motion was driven by individual bevel gears. Radial crank rods, turned in one piece by the cold-iron blacksmiths, and from which the *horses* were suspended, generally imparted 2½ oscillations per complete revolution of the roundabout.

Crown Centre

part of the top centre assembly—the inverted truncated cone, made up of richly decorated shutters that spring from the drum. The number of shutters depends on the number of radial sections in the spinning frame.

Cyclodrome

see under Velocipede and Tandem Bicycles.

Cyclone

see under Twist.

Dancing Machine

a special name given to the Cakewalk developed by Thos. Walker of Tewkesbury, Glos.
See also under Cakewalk.

Dive Bomber

patented by Eyerly in 1938 (No. 520398), twin cars mounted on a vertical rotating arm, also spinning on their own axes. As the name implies, the sensation of diving and of looping-the-loop is realistically created.

Dobby Horses

also known as the 'Steam Circus' before the introduction of galloping motion, the *horses* were merely hung from the swifts, and only slightly restrained against swinging out—horse irons changed to square section at the base in order to prevent the *horse* from twisting.

Some of the early Dobby sets were hand-propelled.

Savages supplied a 3-Abreast set to showman Saunders in 1872—a hand set with 2 cranks and gearing. In the same

(above) a 3-abreast Dobby set built for showman S. Field in the 1870's (drawing reconstructed from an old lithograph)
(top left) fragment of an old wood block found at Savage's works—date unknown
(top right) a carved Dobby horse made between 1860 and 1874, and later used as a rocking horse by children of the Savage household

157

year, steam-driven sets were supplied to Pettigrove and Mullett, and in 1873 belt-drive sets were made for Stocks and Fintum. There may have been earlier sets than these. Between 1881 and 1891 the following steam-driven 3-abreast Dobby Horses were made—all with centre trucks designed to pass the railway loading gauge. With spinning frame divided into 12 sections, the 36 *horses* were single-seaters, but A. Bates' set had two carriages seating 6 children. The levers or swifts were horizontal (in ' Galloping Horses' they were given a slight inclination) and their height above ground level was only 10 ft 3 in— no platforms were fitted.

> 1881, October for Murphy Bros. (Savage engine No. 254)
> 1882, July for Charles Heal
> 1883, January for A. Bates
> 1885, October for Collyer (Savage engine No. 362)
> 1887, November for Jennings (Savage engine No. 411)
> 1890, January for Breeds (Savage engine No. 486)
> 1891, December for Strickland (Savage engine No. 533) (the sets built for Bates, Jennings and Strickland had revolving centres, mirrored in 10 sections, and lighting was almost certainly by gas).
> 4-abreast Dobby Horses were probably supplied to F. Bailey and W. & S. Hancock, both in 1877, and to Wm. Davies in 1878.

Dodg'em *(above right)*
an amusement device comprising electrically charged ceiling and running floor with dirigible cars.

> The following Patents are relevant:—
> 1921 – No. 177395 (Stoehrer)
> 1922 – No. 208877 (Riehl)
> 1923 – No. 216000 (Riehl, incorporating gear change)

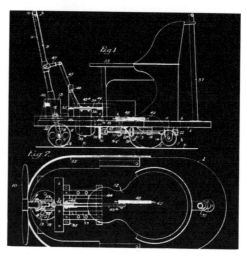

> 1924 – No. 225601 (Lusse Bros. as illustrated)
> 1925 – No. 249981 (Capitelli)
> 1927 – Nos. 301480 and 306059 to 306062 (Lusse)
> 1928 – No. 319649 (Lusse)
> 1930 – No. 346621 (Markey)
> 1932 – No. 386472 (Markey)
> 1934 – No. 445732 (Markey)
> 1937 – No. 489278 (B.M.B.Co.)

Dome
top member in the roundings assembly.

Double Crank Galloper
patented in 1885 by Reynolds & King (No. 15383), the double crank action comprised a mechanism which made the *horses* gallop and their legs move independently. Frank Allchin, eldest son of engine-builder William Allchin, started in business on his own account with Frank Linnel; initially they dealt in second-hand machinery, portable and traction engines, but later they erected a stamping machine in the Midlands Goods Yard, Northampton, in opposition to the established business of William Allchin. Here they built several Double Crank Gallopers for Reynolds & King in or around 1888.

Savage's records show that 4 double-cylinder centre engines were supplied to Allchin, Linnel & Co. in that year.

Driving Levers
another term describing the spokes of the spinning frame. In common usage at the time when Dobby sets were being built, the term almost certainly derived from very early *cartwheel* roundabouts which were propelled by boys pushing on the spokes.

Dropper
bottom member in both roundings and top centre assemblies. Also any decorative element hung below structural units such as rafters or swifts.

Drum
see under Wheel Shutters.

Duo-Directional Roundabout
literally a roundabout offering carriage in two directions. In 1886, Reynolds & King patented a roundabout in which a small locomotive drawing *gondola*-like carriages ran anti-clockwise, and by means of suitable gearing arranged around the centre pole drove the outer ring of 3-abreast ' Galloping Horses' in a clockwise direction. Built by Burrells of Thetford to the order of The Locomotive Merry-go-Round Company Ltd. *c.* 1890, this was probably the first example of a duo-directional machine—see also under Burrell Engines and Roundabouts and *Chronicles of a Country Works* by Ronald H. Clark.

Electric Jumpers
an abbreviated and pop term meaning electric-drive ' Galloping Horses'.

Eli Wheel
see under Ferris Wheel.

Extension Front (above)

in architectural terms the definition given to the entrance to a ride or show. In the illustration there are steps, balustrading and a double row of columns—notice the emphasis given by forward projection and deepening of the roundings.

Ferris Wheel

a power-driven vertical wheel, steel-framed and with freely-pivoted passenger-carrying cars mounted at the extremities. Named after its inventor G. W. G. Ferris, this amusement device is also known as 'Big Wheel' or 'Eli Wheel'.

Flea Circus

an exhibition of performing (human) fleas.

Flying Coaster

a ride of the 1960's comprising circular track with a steep hump and fast moving cars driven round it by a spider frame. Considerable momentum, combined with the sudden obstacle of the hump, propels the cars upwards into space, and the gravitational descent is softened only slightly by pneumatics.

Flying Machine

in general terms, any riding device simulating flight—there have been many.

Specifically a ride built by Thos. Walker of Tewkesbury and described in their catalogue as follows :—

. . . The ride on this machine is a correct reproduction of the gliding, swooping movement of an aeroplane. The cars are suspended from above so that the machine can be driven at a very high velocity which adds to the excitement . . . . A continuous platform, with steps leading up all round, is fitted so that passengers can mount . . . or alight at any point.'

With 8 cars each carrying 8 passengers the ride could be either steam or electric drive—the price about £1,100.

In 1889 Savages built an 'Aerial Flight' machine for Nicholson : an inverted spiral 24 ft high gave a gravitational ride in suspended cars.

Flying Pigs (below)

a variant of the Platform Galloper having *pigs* instead of *horses*, and *waltzing balloons*. The illustration shows Reuben Holdsworth's set at Hull Fair in 1908—notice the counter-clockwise direction of movement, and the unusual design of roundings.

Flying Saucers

developed from the Wheel this ride has 14 cars constructed in the assumed form of *flying saucers*. Mounted on a turntable, the wheel makes 4 revolutions for each complete revolution of the base.

Because of its size—the wheel measures 50 ft and the base 30 ft in diameter—the Flying Saucer machine is not generally regarded as transportable, although it is on the continent. See also *Further Notes on the Development of Fairground Machinery* by P. W. Bradley —*The Engineer* 22nd March 1957.

(left) Extension Front to Pat Collins 'Speedway'

(below) Reuben Holdsworth's 'Flying Pigs and Balloons' at Hull Fair, 1908

Freak Show
an exhibition of human or animal freaks, now declining in popularity.

Gaff
defined, perhaps unkindly, by Webster as follows :—
' Slang, Eng. (where " fish " or " suckers " are gaffed). A cheap place of amusement.' Specifically the stance or show-ground where fairs are held.

Gag Card *(below)*
the illustration is self-explanatory.

Gallopers
generically a roundabout with *animals* made to gallop by some mechanical means. The terms 2-, 3- or 4-abreast merely qualify the number of *animals* arranged side by side (see Abreast).

Garniture
a term, now obsolete, meaning embellishment; hence a garniture rail was the frame from which additional decorations were hung.

Garter
in top motion switchbacks a circular band that formed the rim of the spinning frame and, as such, restrained the complex of swifts, sullivans and stays. Usually emphasised by carving and inset mirrors, the Garter was also an important decorative feature.

Gate
a component in the sub-frame assembly designed to carry platforms and, in the case of the switchback, undulating tracks. The use of uprights and diagonal bracing led to an inevitable association of ideas.

Ghost Train
a ride and show combined. At discreet intervals, dummy trains running on an energised rail—carrying no more than two passengers—penetrate the darkened booth. A labyrinth of hair-raising spectacles, optical tricks and sudden cloying tactility await them.

Glide
see under Alpine Glide and Paramount Glide.

Gipsy Lee *(below)*
commonly the fortune-teller's booth—there have been countless Gipsy Lee's and no doubt there are many more to come.

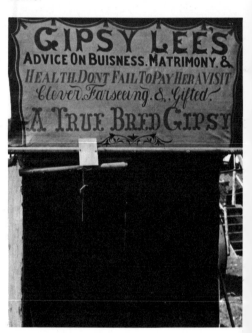

Golden Flame Lamps
an early form of electric carbon arc lighting introduced *c.* 1900 and giving high-intensity spot sources.

Gondola
generically a roundabout car, and specifically an ornate carriage, decorated in the Baroque style and used in early switchbacks.

Gravity Ride
see under Big Dipper.

Haunted Castle (above)

the terms 'Crazy House' and 'Frankenstein's Castle' are roughly synonymous. Insatiable curiosity is the draw—some diabolical mechanical effects, a few missing steps and the inevitable wind machine, are perhaps a fit recompense.

Helter Skelter (right)

also known as Alpine Slip, Glide and Mat Slide : basically a tower-like structure contained within an unwinding spiral chute. The tower encloses a staircase by means of which the riders climb to the top of the chute. Sitting on individual mats they then descend—by gravity.

Hoop-La

generically any round stall, but specifically a game with hoops in which the player has to ring his prize.

Horse Irons (right)

the rods on which roundabout *horses* are suspended.

Hurricane Jets

a fast ride simulating flight, with the hiss of pneumatics evocative of jet engines. Originally built to a German design, the angle of inclination of each of the 12 cars

can be controlled by the riders. Compressed air cylinders and pistons that lift individual swifts, and an electric motor with the necessary gearing, can all be mounted on a centre truck.

Jack and Jill Glide

otherwise known as Mountain Glide. A gravity ride comprising a continuous chute supported on gates of diminishing height, and having a power-driven continuous belt—fitted with seats—to carry the riders to the top platform.

Jazz Ride

a name calculated to rejuvenate the ageing Cakewalk.

Jets

see under Hurricane Jets.

Joint

in slang terms 'a gathering place', but on the fairground it is used as a generic term for any form of portable side-show of the *ground booth* variety. *Walk-Up* shows, which have a raised platform for performers, are not so described.

Jollity Farm

another name for the Ark.

Jolly Jersey Bounce

in contemporary dance idiom yet another name for the Cakewalk.

Jolly Tubes

a pair of counter-rotating tubes or barrels through which paying members of the public have to walk. An amusement device that originated in France, Charles W. R. Thurston was the first showman to present a set in this country.

Joy Wheel

rather more a challenge than a joy ride, this revolving conical disc was extremely difficult to stay on—indeed there were usually more spectators than there were riders. Of short-lived popularity, and apparently built only by Savages, very few of these machines were ever on tour. The following list, compiled from some old drawings and not necessarily complete, suggests a cessation of production after less than 2 years :—

1910	W. & S. Hancock	50ft diam.
	H. Wallis	,,
	J. Evans, Jnr.	,,
	Swales Bolesworth	,,
	A. Ball	48ft diam.
	C. Thurston	46ft diam.
1911	J. W. Waddington	50ft diam.
	W. H. Marshall	,,

Juvenile *(below)*
generally a children's roundabout, or other ride, scaled down and slowed down, for the enjoyment and safety of children.

King Pole
the centre mast, or masts, of a circus 'Big Top'.

Lessee
generally refers to the showman or group of showmen who hold the lease for a particular fairground. The Lessee, or his Manager, is responsible for allocating

ground to the Tenants, organising the layout and ensuring the proper conduct of the fair. Individual rents are collected from the Tenants, and the Lessee pays to the owner of the ground an agreed lump sum. For example, in the 1920's showman Lessee John Murphy paid a rent of 1,000 guineas on behalf of the North-Eastern Roundabout Proprietors for 3 days on Newcastle Town Moor.

Lever
see under Driving Levers.

Lighthouse Slip or Lighthouse Helter Skelter
so called because of the similarity in form —see under Helter Skelter.

Looper
a roundabout, the cars of which are constructed in the form of miniature wheels—see also under Allchin, William, in Appendix II. The Looper, a modern device apparently based on this patent, was presented by John Collins in the late 1940's—it enjoyed only limited success.

Machine
any form of mechanically-propelled riding device. Thus a Machine Position on any

fairground is the site occupied by a roundabout or other form of joy ride.

Mat Slide
see under Helter Skelter.

Meteorite *(below)*
a modern device based on the principle of centrifugal force. The wheel has cage-like compartments at the rim and once set in motion the axis is inclined until this wheel is near vertical—for riders contained in the cages it is altogether a breath-taking experience.

Hundreds of electric lamps, emphasising the structure and delineating a 6-pointed star, give a spectacular effect at night. It is also one of the most compact rides on tour.

Mirror Maze
as the name implies, a labyrinth of mirrors, plane and distorting—with some clear glass thrown in to add to the confusion. Raucous amusement for the family, but not a good money-spinner, there are very few of these shows on tour.

Mont Blanc
see under Airways.

Monte Carlo Rally
see under Brooklands Speedway.

Moon Rocket *(above)*
invented by the late Charles Openshaw of Reading, this heavy machine is slowly disappearing from the fairground. As originally conceived, a circle of rocket-shaped cars are driven, at some speed, round an inclined circular track. The height of the trestles and the restraint necessary against centrifugal force involve a considerable weight of framing—as can be seen from the illustration.

Subsequent modifications include the substitution of freely pivoted cars and attempted rejuvenation by names like 'Space Cruisers,' 'Space Ships' and 'Strato-Rockets'.

The following Patents are relevant:—
1888 – No. 4346 (Green)
1936 – No. 482000 (Openshaw).
George Green's design included a musician's gallery.

Monorail
a rare member of the switchback family with a part circle of tub-shaped cars driven round an undulating track. The static enclosure is usually constructed with an open top.

The following Patent is relevant:—
1928 — No. 320758 (Traver)

Mop Fair
a fair which became associated with the hiring of domestic servants—see also Appendix IV.

Motor-Car Scenic
an early electric-drive switchback with a circle of dummy motor cars as the vehicle, and having a profusion of scenery, mechanical and lighting effects in the centre.

Motor-Cycle Speedway
see under Ark.

Mountain Glide *(above right)*
see under 'Jack and Jill' Glide.

Mountain Ponies *(illustration page 164)*
also known as Switchback Gallopers and Switchback Horses—a hybrid derived from Platform Gallopers and the switchback.

The undulating tramways were generally arranged to form 2 hills and 2 valleys, 3ft or 3ft 6in rise, with a spinning top divided into 12, 14 or 16 sections.

The early machines had segmental platforms mounted with *horses*, *cockerels* or *ostriches* 3-abreast. A mechanism similiar to that devised for the Platform Galloper gave an independent rocking motion to each *animal*. After 1891, diameters increased so that a 4th ring of *still horses* could be mounted on the inside. Alternatively one or two sections of *animals* were left out, and rocking *boats*, *chariots* or *swan cars* put in their place.

As with the switchback, motion was imparted by a complex of sullivans, stays and pulling rods.

Patented by Green in 1889 (No. 6140), this remarkable machine was the forerunner of today's Noah's Ark.

The following list has been compiled

163

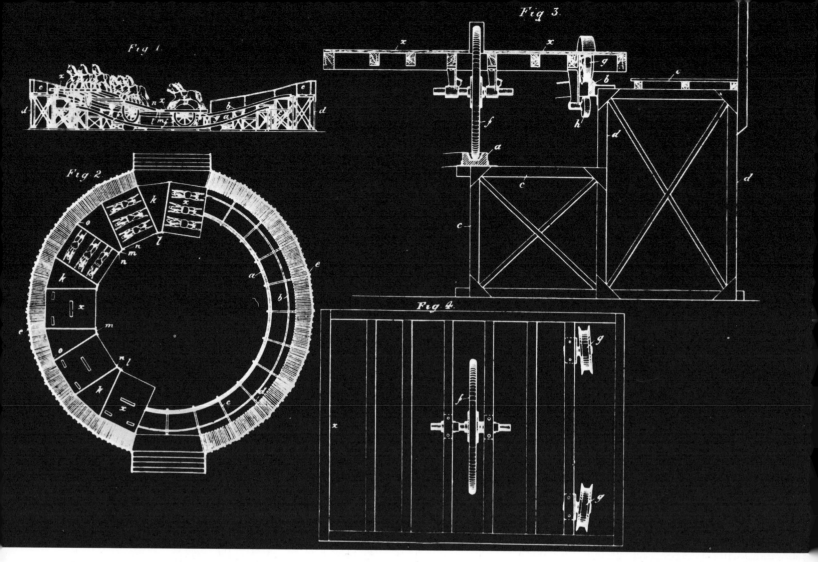

Fig 1.

Fig 2.

Fig 3.

Fig 4.

from fragmentary information on drawings found at Savage's Works:—

1888 for showman Speckstadt—a prototype machine, or conversion of a standard Platform Galloper.

1889 Richardson Brothers.
Pat Collins—subsequently sold to Siebold.
Walter Murphy—14 sections, 3-rail wooden tramway, 51ft 8in in diameter—spinning frame 45ft 2in, with 3ft 6in rise.
John Collins.
J. Wilmot.
W. Davis.

J. White.

1890 George Green—fitted with special steel channel trams in 1896.

1891 Mitchell & Sons.
W. Mitchell—4-abreast with the inside *horse* mounted on an outrigger.

c.1892 Mme. Willemsen.

1893 Speckstadt—4-abreast with 42 mechanical *horses*, 14 *still horses* and 2 cars.
Measuring 54ft in diameter—the spinning top 46ft 3in, this machine had gas lighting—5 *trees* each with 8 branches on a ring

23ft in diameter. The sections mounted with *horses* had pillars and handrails, cased with brass, on the inside.

Mousetown
an exhibition of performing mice.

Movable Dwellings Bill (1910)
a parliamentary bill introduced by George Smith and proposing legislation to control sanitation and education of van-dwellers. An Inspector of Nuisances was designated. That the Bill was defeated was largely due to the vigorous efforts of

the United Kingdom Van Dwellers' Protection Association.

The Public Health Act of 1936 contained the 'Showmen's Charter' giving protection to travelling showmens' caravans both on the fairground and in winter quarters.

Mystic Swing

sometimes known as the Rib Tickler, an invention attributed to showman Randall Williams—riders entered a completely dark box which, being pivoted, was then swung back and forth by the attendants. A few of these are still on tour—mostly in the north of England.

Noah's Ark

see under Ark.

Octopus

A riding device of the *elemental spoked wheel* variety and, apart from a faintly evocative motion, bearing little resemblance to the 8-legged aquatic.

In his Patent dated 1936 (No. 485869) Lee Ulric Eyerly describes his invention in part as follows:—

'It has previously been proposed in amusement appliances of the see-saw type to impart an up and down movement to vehicles or seats of passengers by mounting them on a see-saw bar, and at the same time to rotate the see-saw bar or board about its centre.

'In the present invention, a plurality of radial arms are rotatable about a vertical axis . . .

'Each of the arms . . . is hinged with respect to the axis of rotation, and a crank pin is associated with the revolvable arms near the axis of rotation and is connected with the arms through connecting rods whereby upon rotation of the crank pin and the arms at different speeds or in different directions a rotary and rocking movement is imparted to the arms.'

Like the Meteorite, a spectacular ride when seen at night, with hundreds of electric lamps delineating the spokes and a circle of mirrors at the centre.

Organ Engine *(left)*

an auxiliary engine for driving mechanical organs. Like the steam centre engine, it was pioneered by Sidney George Soame of Marsham, Norfolk, but further developed and commercialised by Frederick Savage.

Normally mounted well forward on the boiler of the centre engine, it was coupled to the organ by flat belt drive. The illustration shows a Savage No. 4 Organ Engine (late type) *c.* 1922—notice the centrifugal governors that ensured an even tempo.

Over-the-Tops *(below left)*

a variant of the swing: the pivoted carriage always remaining horizontal it was possible to go *over the top* without falling out.

Pagoda Top

a Platform Galloper built by Savages, apparently to the special order of showman J. Wilmot. Later the ride was sold to George Green, and finally to Coney Island, New York. The Pagoda Top, formed by framing external to the tilt, was unique and, almost certainly, never repeated. Its weight was quite a problem because once in motion it tended to act like a fly-wheel. This made the machine difficult to stop as hard braking would snap the swifts.

Panatrope

successor to the mechanical organ—gramophone turntables, amplifier and loudspeakers relaying noisy pop records and, intermittently, the commanding voice of the riding master.

Paramount Glide
see under Helter Skelter.

Paramount Speedway
see under Ark.

Paratrooper *(below)*
also known as Paratrip—a wheel revolving at an oblique angle supporting freely pivoted 2-seater carriages which can either be rocked by their occupants or hang vertically. An *umbrella* suspended above each carriage resembles—perhaps faintly—a parachute.

Pied Poudre
Court of, sometimes referred to as Court of Pie Powder—a Court of Pedlars, from *pied poudre* meaning dusty feet. Set up at ancient trading fairs, this court would settle differences arising between the fleeting population of merchants. In a sense, the present-day Showmen's Guild carries on the tradition, acting as arbitrator in the matter of disputes between travelling showmen.

Pitch Getter
one who prepares the *pitch*—in colloquial terms a spieler who, by means of enticing words, draws a crowd.

Platform Galloper *(above)*
a roundabout in which galloping motion was imparted to the *animals* by eccentrics on the main platform-carrying wheels. The *animals* were mounted on two stiff rods—one at each end—and these were connected to a pair of cranks on the main axle. As the machine was set in motion, riders experienced a rocking movement.

One of the first Platform Gallopers was supplied to Pat Collins—known as 'The Boston Riding School' the illustration shows this set at King's Lynn Mart, *c.* 1890.

The following Patent is relevant:—
1885 – No. 12090 (Savage)

Platform Slide
a device in 'Galloping Horse' roundabouts (overhead crank motion) allowing *horse* and rider to swing out as the machine gathers momentum. Horse irons passed through radial slots in the platform and into a guide plate that ensured equi-distant swinging out in 2-, 3- and 4-abreast sets.

The following Patent is relevant:—
1891 – No. 1116 (Savage)

Poultry Farm
particular name for a Platform Galloper having a profusion of *cockerels* instead of *horses*. George Green's '4-abreast Giant Bantams' were a particularly fine example.

Punter
literally a gambler, but in less harsh fairground terms one who participates in the various games.

Quarterings *(facing page above)*
in structural terms, the ties between spokes, or swifts, of the spinning frame. Generally arranged concentrically, in overhead crank motion roundabouts there are bushings mid-span to support the crank rods.

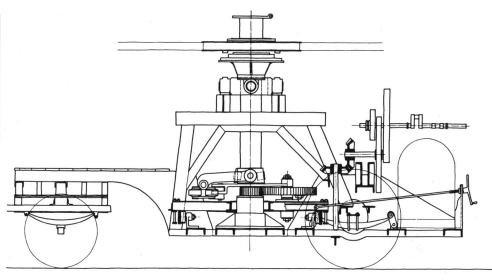

Racing Cockerels

as an alternative to *horses*, double-seater *cockerels* were fitted to Platform and top motion Gallopers, and the name 'Racing Cockerels' substituted.

Rafters

those structural members giving support to the canvas awning or tilt: in the case of a spinning frame or circular enclosure, rafters would be arranged in a radial pattern.

Razzle Dazzle *(above right)*

also known as Aerial Novelty and Whirligig:

A composite spinning frame driven from beneath having radial seats on a flat platform and an eccentric on the axis causing it to tilt up and down as the frame revolved.

Although a most ingenious mechanism, and years ahead of its time, the ride was not popular. Existing records indicate that Savage-built Razzle Dazzles were supplied only to Pat Collins, John Collins and to Mitchells, and one was probably exported.

Nor was it popular with the driver who, being under the platform, had no way of knowing how great a load he was carrying, nor whether any emergencies had arisen above.

The following Patents are relevant:—

    1893 – No. 6635 (Savage)
    1897 – No. 13735 (Hurst)

An improved version, built by Howcrofts of West Hartlepool, was supplied to Joe Wingate, and to Northampton showmen Relph & Pedley.

Rib Tickler

see under Mystic Swing.

Ride

generally any form of mechanically-driven, passenger-carrying amusement device, otherwise referred to as riding device, machine, or in the case of a specific roundabout type—set.

Riding Master

one who controls or owns a ride.

Rock an' Roll

a further alternative name for the Cakewalk, but also a modification to the Waltzer—known as the 'Rock an' Roll' attachment, which levelled the track between two hills and caused a degree of syncopation in the movement.

Rodeo Switchback

presumably an alternative name for Mountain Ponies, although in recent years it has come to be known as an Ark with a preponderance of *horses* mounted on the platforms. In the latter case, one of the finest examples belongs to Culine Bros.—travellers in the north of England.

Roll Ups

a game of questionable skill where an apparently arbitrary score of numbers secures one of a range of prizes. Four or six balls are rolled up an inclined board to find lodgment in circular holes, each one of which has a numerical value.

Rotor

the antithesis of the Joy Wheel: an amusement device comprising a revolving drum with inverted conical bottom—as the drum gathers momentum riders are flung against the walls, and there they stick while the bottom is gradually lowered. There are usually more spectators than riders.

    The following Patent is relevant:—

      1949 – No. 659605 (Hoffmeister)

Rounding Board

a continuous label to the spinning frame: in architectural terms a fascia which forms the rim of the wheel. See also under Roundings.

Roundings *(right)*

the fascia as a composite assembly including rounding boards and dropper and, in more elaborate machines, the upper component of dome.

    Static enclosure machines eventually had deeper roundings, sometimes cut about in giant fret-work patterns to represent tropical foliage, sometimes flat-painted very much in the Pre-Raphaelite tradition; in both cases constituent parts, i.e. rounding board, dropper and dome, became obscured.

Round 'Un

any circular joint or stall.

Runaway Mop

generally held some two weeks after the Mop Fair, dissatisfied customers could here trade in domestics and labourers who had proved unsatisfactory.

Satellite *(below)*

otherwise known as Trabant: a ride which owes much to Savage's Razzle Dazzle, and rather less to Eyerly's Octopus. The wheel has cars for 40 adults or 60 teenagers—at least 800 riders per hour. Like the Razzle Dazzle, the axis is tilted once the wheel has gathered momentum, but this complete mechanism is itself mounted on a turntable. Replete with fluorescent lighting, colour-impregnated fibreglass, and hydraulics throughout, this American importation is the very last word in joyriding.

    The Satellite is manufactured under licence by Ivan Bennett Engineering Co. Ltd. of Long Eaton, Nottingham.

Savage Bottom

so-called because of the origin of design

—by Frederick Savage—this refers to the 3-rail system for switchbacks—a system subsequently adopted by other round-about builders who accordingly paid a royalty for it. One such firm was Orton, Sons & Spooner, who built a great many switchbacks using the Savage Bottom. See also under Compensating Rail.

Savage Sparkler

a portable electric light engine : Savage-built reciprocating steam-engine coupled by belt drive to a dynamo. The 'Sparkler' was intended to be horse-drawn, and because of its weight—about 7 tons—and also its extreme sensitivity it was never very popular. Indeed its un-popularity inhibited the use of electricity on the fairground until the showmen's traction engine emerged.

See also under Dickinson in Appendix II.

Savage Motion (right)

refers to the superior gearing devised by Savages for driving overhead cranks in the 'Galloping Horse' roundabout.

Scenic

a generic term for electrically driven switchbacks having a profusion of scenery.

Sea-on-Land

an early steam-drive roundabout having six or eight dummy yachts, complete with awnings, propelled about a circular track. The mechanism imparted a rolling and pitching motion.

Records indicate that only a dozen or so of these machines were built. The following showmen appear to have ordered them :—

Twigdon, P. Collins, Murphy, Aspland, Studt, Duffield, Davies, Siebold & Otto, Mitchell, Hill & Son, Nokes & Rix, and Green.

Fairground Architecture

The following Patents are relevant:—
  1880 – No. 1812 (Sanger and Savage)
  1881 – No. 5375 (Savage)

Side stuff
a colloquial term meaning a linear arrangement of side-shows.

Sheet
another name for Coconut Shy, *shy* meaning 'to throw sideways with a jerk'.

Shooter
a Shooting Gallery or Range, generally presented as a side-show.

Skid
see under Swirl.

Sky Wheels
introduced at the Festival Gardens, Battersea, London, in 1951—a ponderous machine with two 25 ft diameter wheels revolving at opposite ends of a centrally pivoted and rotating arm. Like Flying Saucers, too large a machine to be economically transportable.

Sleeper
component in the sub-frame of machines, booths and joints: that member which transmits the load from frames, trestles and the like, to the ground. Always requiring to be carefully levelled and, in the case of circular static enclosures, to be set out in a radial pattern its correct alignment is absolutely essential.

Space Cruisers
a more recent name for, and in certain cases a variant of the Moon Rocket—see also Strato-Rockets.

Speedway
a loose term which could refer either to an

Ark—mounted with *motor-cycles,* or to a Monte Carlo Rally.

Spider Frame
as the name and context imply, a revolving frame with fixed, radial arms—a wheel without a rim: the core of roundabouts like the Swirl, Octopus and Jets.

Spinner *(above)*
a game of chance now declining in popularity: in essence a revolving emblem with electrical commutator and flashing lights illuminating the names of horses, football teams, film stars. When the spinner comes to rest, the light then showing denotes the winning ticket.

A fierce roundabout motif, bare bulbs and glittering swag, the Spinner was always a good draw. London showman George Pickard still travels with his celebrated 'Boadicea Spinner', but others are fast being supplanted by 'Bingo'.

Spinning Frame *(facing page)*
prime mover in the roundabout: the spoked wheel that impels motion. In the case of the 'Galloping Horse' roundabout, the composite of swifts and

quarterings, crank rods and tilt rods, and the decorated rim of the rounding boards.

In the case of top motion switchbacks, more robust wooden swifts, brass encased sullivans, stays and pulling rods—a complex of driving forces and reactions contained by a garter which was also a prime embellishment.

Modern switchbacks, like the Ark, have steel swifts which are also rubber-wheeled axles driven round the undulating track. Hinged segmental platforms, pinned to the axles, carry *animals* and *chariots*.

Spinning Top

the type-name given to any switchback propelled by an elevated spinning frame, and in which this spinning frame is expressed. Conversely top motion switchbacks, contained within a static enclosure, were known as fixed top switchbacks.

Statute

affectionately known in the East Midlands as ' Statty '—a fair originally associated with the hire of domestic and farm labour.

Steam Circus

the name invented by William Sanger of Margate, Kent, for steam-drive Dobbies. See under Dobbies.

Steam Swings

a loose term that has become associated with Steam Yachts, but more precisely it referred to an arrangement of 6 or 8 Swing Boats with vertical steam engine in the centre. This power drive could be harnessed to individual boats by the friction induced by pulling on a rope. Until quite recently showman John Pullen travelled such a set. The following Patent is relevant :—

    1886 – No. 10726 (Reynolds & Everitt)

Steam Yachts *(illustration page 172)*

a giant Swing Boat or pair of such boats coupled by chain-drive chain to a portable steam engine. Special gearing, known because of its shape as the *rabbit*, prevented the piston from overrunning a dead centre and thereby the boat from swinging over the top.

The subject of an early Patent (1888 — No. 9375) by William Cartwright and Henry Cracknell, where the motion was imparted to a single boat by connecting rod, the idea achieved maturity in Cartwright's design of 1894 (Patent No. 15138).

The following sets—each with a pair of boats—were built by Savages of King's Lynn. Almost certainly the list is incomplete :—

    1895 – J. Collins.
    1897 – J. Richards.
    1899 – C. Baker.
    1901 – Waddington (now Henry Lee's)
    1902 – Mrs. Ross.
    1910 – M. Kanner (France).
    1914 – J. W. Waddington.
    1915 – F. Gray.
    1920 – P. Collins Jnr.
    1921 – J. Ling.
    1921 – T. Kaye.
    1922 – Hibbert Bros.
    1928 – Mrs. Hoadley.

In addition to Harry Lee's set, Ling's are still on tour but with drive converted to diesel engine. A single boat, formerly Ryan's of Lancashire, is now owned in preservation by Commander Baldock of Liphook, Hants—driven by a converted Burrell steam-roller it is much of an oddity.

In their heyday Steam Yachts cost around £1,500. At Hull Fair there have been as many as five sets at one time, but a number of unfortunate accidents marred their success. Compared with other old rides that have survived they are by far the most exciting.

Still Horse Roundabout

a form of Carousel in which fixed *horses*, sometimes in galloping stance, are mounted on the platform.

Strato-Rockets

a variant of the Moon Rocket in which the cars are pivoted and can be rocked by their riders.

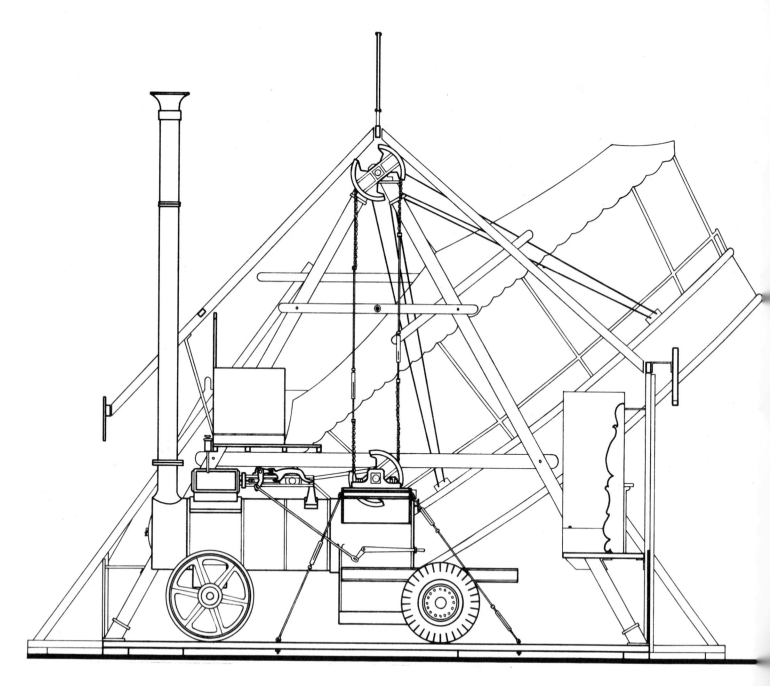

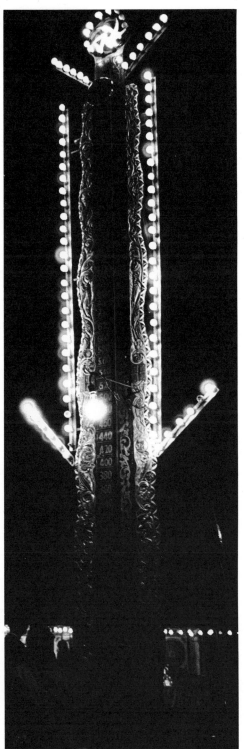

Striker *(left)*

a test of strength and of skill: to ring the bell involves a good deal of both. The illustration is self-explanatory.

Sullivan

vertical member in the draw-bar assembly of top motion switchbacks—see also under Spinning Frame.

The story is told of one of Savage's workmen who, during building-up operations, was knocked unconscious as the spinning frame was turned on a section. Told what had happened when he came to, the workman replied: 'Blimey, I thought it must 'ave been Sullivan '—meaning John L. Sullivan, then World Heavyweight Champion. The name has stuck.

Swag

in showmen's language the collective name for prizes given on the various stalls.

Swifts

formerly known as driving levers, the spokes of the spinning frame.

Swing Boat *(below)*

literally the simplest form of ride which probably originated in primeval antiquity. With larger boats suspended between sturdy 'A' frames, an arrangement of ropes enabled riders to swing higher merely by pulling on them. Deavin and Sutton's Patent No. 401 of 1864 is relevant.

Nowadays a 'Set of Boats', or 'Park Swings' as they are sometimes called, usually comprises a range of 6 or 8 boats side by side with a crude form of friction brake under each. With this the ride can be abruptly curtailed and the next paying customer installed.

The illustration shows in the foreground a giant boat swung from underneath by 2 attendants, an unusual form of mechanically propelled Over-Boat (see also Over-the-Tops), and the more conventional Swing Boats in the background.

Swirl or Swish

a modern ride based on the Whip, but with a circular spider frame, freely-pivoted cars each with a brake pedal

controlling the pivot, and a flat steel floor contained within a static enclosure. The following Patents are relevant :—

1929 – No. 328770 (Thurston, Thurston & Lakin), and
No. 333803 (Giraud)

Switchback

a circular ride comprising a plurality of cars driven round an undulating track. See also under Ark, Autodrome, Caterpillar and Scenic. The following Patent is relevant :—

1887 – No. 12361 (Welburn)

Tandem Novelty

a Velocipede roundabout having two-seater *bicycles*.

Tenant

any showman who rents ground for his amusements from a fairground Lessee.

Tilt

the canvas awning to any amusement device, presumably so-called because of the angle of inclination designed to act as a water-shed.

Tilt Rods

those structural members that carry the tilt—see also under Rafters.

Tipping Jets

a development of Vampire Jets where the centre pole is tipped forward during the ride giving the riders a sensation of diving.

Tober

the total complex of the fairground—its planning, organisation, and induced atmosphere. More specifically, the layout of rides, booths and joints.

Toboggan

a form of gravity ride now obsolete.

Top Centre

that complex of ornate shutters masking the hub, or cheese, and gearing of the spinning frame. Generally in the form of an inverted truncated cone, rich decoration and the glitter from numerous cut glass mirrors make this a focal point in the roundabout.

Top Motion

a type-name for any roundabout in which revolution and compounded movements are imparted by an elevated spinning frame. Objectively the term refers to the mechanism imparting such motion.

Trabant

the original American name for the Satellite—see under Satellite.

Traction Centre *(below)*

a specially-designed steam road locomotive adaptable for driving top motion roundabouts. With hornplates extended upwards, an elevated platform carried cheese and gearing. In Savage-built engines the roundabout drive was by dog clutch and bevel gears off the crankshaft. An auxiliary flue acted as an extension centre pole—see illustration.

Originally intended to simplify transportation problems, making one engine do double-duty, the Traction Centre failed because of the incompatibility of these two duties. The following Patents are relevant :—

1880 – No. 3937 (Savage)
1895 – No. 21403 (Burrell)

Trams

literally a portable tramway, set up on the ground, pre-levelled, and on to which centre trucks and organ trucks were winched.

Trestle

see under Gate.

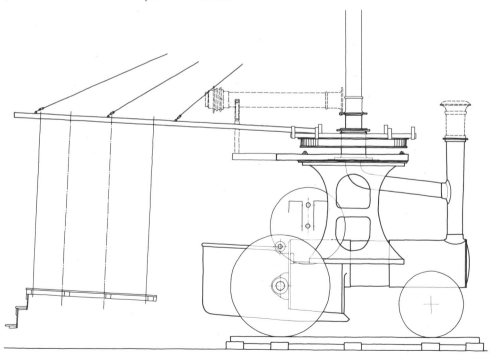

Tunnel of Love

almost any amusement device incorporating a ride through a darkened tunnel—the connotations are obvious. Thus the 'Tunnel of Love Autodrome' is merely a standard Autodrome with half of the track shrouded by a tunnel.

The following Patents have some relevance :—

    1899 — No. 19258
    1904 — No. 27848
    1906 — No. 9277

Tunnel Railway

A circular *railway* with a real steam locomotive drawing six carriages, and a tunnel covering half of the track. One showman described it thus :—

' a young railway, Dover to Callis in ten minutes, three times, and all for a penny ' (extract from *A Parish on Wheels* by Rev. J. Howard Swinstead).

Records are incomplete, but Tunnel Railways were probably supplied by Savages to the following showmen :—

P. Collins, W. Davies, W. H. Marshall, T. Tuby, Thurston & Barker, Symonds, Dodsworth & Barnsley, Read & Bailey.

Turret Gear

the vertical extension and overhead gearwork fitted to the traction centre.

Twist

also known as Cyclone, Whirlwind Twist and, in America, Scrambler. An elevated 4-arm spider frame with revolving shafts suspended from each arm carrying smaller spider frames each mounted with four cars.

A further development in the *wheels within wheels* concept, the Twist is a comparatively new roundabout. Usually constructed with an open top, one or two have been built with radial sleepers, a slatted timber platform, rafters and tilt.

United Kingdom Van Dwellers Protection Association

founded in 1889 to protect the interests of travelling showmen, the Association had, at one time, 21 famous showmen as Vice-Presidents, 3 solicitors, 8 chaplains and a Parliamentary Agent. Its Presidents have included Sanger, Bostock and Pat Collins.

Reconstituted in the early 1900's as a Trade Protection Association for Showmen, it later became known as the Showmen's Guild. See also under Movable Dwellings Bill.

Vampire Jets *(above)*

a development of Hurricane Jets where the centre cheese can be given a rise and fall motion. Using compressed air—a single cylinder concealed within the centre shaft—the riding master would normally give two lifts during the course of a ride. On account of this mechanism the maximum elevation of individual cars could be as much as 29 ft.

Again based on a German design, Vampire Jets were built under licence by Lang Wheels Ltd. of Hillingdon Heath. The first set to be presented in this country was specially commissioned by Botton Bros.

Velocipede *(below)*

based on the pedal cycle, perhaps the most ancient of all mechanical roundabouts. Early sets had a single row of *cycles*, a grooved circular track and radial ties slotted into a cheese. The speed attained depended on the vigour of the patrons, but the riding master could apply a brake at the centre. The illustration shows a set built by Frederick Savage in the 1860's.

Also in the 1860's, Savage built a 2-abreast Velocipede—48 *cycles*—and this set was driven by a portable steam engine. Although these were Mr. Savage's own inventions—claims W. Sparkes in his *Biography of Frederick Savage*—he neglected to patent them.

Cycle Roundabouts 1875

It may be of more than passing interest to note that implicit in the manually propelled Velocipede was the *free-wheel* mechanism, and Savage made his own patterns for this—they still exist today.

According to old and possibly incomplete records, the following were among the first showmen to take delivery of steam-drive Velocipede machines :—

1870 – Hough.

Charles Bugg.

Pettigrove.

1871 – Francis Bailey—16 *cycle* set.

George Aspland—2-abreast 20 set.

Kilbride—2-abreast 20 set.

1872 – Chamberlain & Briggs—2-abreast 20 set.

Sanger.

Armitage.

(the sets supplied to Bailey, Aspland and Kilbride were illuminated by gas). It is possible that 3-abreast and even 4-abreast Velocipedes were built at a later date.

The following Patents have some relevance :—

1885 – No. 13125 (Francis & Francis)

1896 – No. 17109 (Collins & Savage)

Wall of Death

introduced in the 1920's, a spectacular and very dangerous performance by motor cyclists who, relying on centrifugal force, drive round the inside walls of a vertical cylinder. Paying spectators peer over the top rim and toss coins down into the arena.

The 'Globe of Death', a similar display in a spherical cage with open bottom, is even more dangerous.

Lady drivers, and wild beasts carried on the pillion, were not surprisingly an even greater draw.

Waltzer

a member of the switchback family having freely-pivoted tub-shaped cars mounted on the undulating platform. Dance movements simulated by mechanics were pioneered, perhaps rather crudely, in the Cakewalk. The Everitt and Burrell roundabout was a good deal more sophisticated. Mr. Jackson's 'Waltzing Discs' emerged in 1919, and some ten years later the Waltzer, substantially in the form we know it today, made its debut.

The following Patents are relevant :—

1881 – No. 5433 (Everitt & Burrell)

1920 – No. 139348 (Jackson)

1929 – No. 328633 (Jackson)

1933 – No. 409905 (Lakin & Thurston)

Waltzing Balloon

an ornate passenger-carrying *globe* fitted to roundabouts of the Platform Galloper variety—see also under Flying Pigs. By means of a suitable gearing the *globe* turned on its own axis as the platform revolved.

Water Dodg'em

Apparently originated in Vienna, an aquatic amusement apparatus based on the Dodg'em car, having an electrically charged ceiling structure, but using water as 'earth'. Suitable trolley poles were fitted to individual boats, but clearly the application of this ride was more suited to permanent amusement parks. Two ladies from Orpington—Rebecca Burrow and Mary Jane Hill—developed the design in this country.

The following Patents are relevant :—

1929 – No. 343541 (Thoerig)

1931 – No. 377000 and 379095 (Burrow & Hill)

Wembley Whirl *(below)*

also known as the Devil's Disc.

A very fast machine, reputed to be

German-built and comprising an inclined spinning frame with seats at the rim—facing inwards.

Wheel
see under Ferris Wheel.

Wheel'em In
a game in many ways similar to Roll-ups except that here the balls run down a gently inclined board and come to rest in slots instead of circular apertures.

The game can also be played with pennies rolled down a chute on to a squared table. Prizes, usually in cash, depend on the numerical value of the square in which the penny lands. But if it overlaps with another square no prize is given.

Wheel Shutters
as the name implies—decorated shutters enclosing a wheel, usually the centre drum of a roundabout.

In the case of 'Gallopers', the cheese wheel and overhead gearwork are masked by drum droppers.

Wheely Whirly
see under Joy Wheel. This complex machine probably derived from the Whirlygig (not to be confused with Whirligig) of 1891, and was re-named Wheely Whirly in 1895. Three revolving discs, 18 ft in diameter, were pivoted about a heavy spinning frame—the plane of motion being inclined some 20 degrees above horizontal. The absence of seats, and a sliding door mentioned in the specification, suggest that it was intended as a *riding spectacle* rather like the Joy Wheel.

Showman Jacob Studt apparently took delivery of a modified version which had the discs mounted on rollers.

Whip
invented by Wm. Mangels; the American

forerunner of the Swirl.

The following Patent is relevant:—
1914 – No 18743.

Patent rights for Great Britain were purchased by Fred Green of Glasgow who had the machines manufactured and installed at various Amusement Parks.

Whirligig
see under Razzle Dazzle. Unlike the terms *Merry-go-Round* and *Roundabout*, which are comparatively modern, Whirligig is used by Shakespeare—*Twelfth Night*, Act V, Scene i: 'And thus the whirligig of time brings in his revenges.'

Womp
a key transitional ride between the Whip and the Swirl.

World's Smallest Woman
—can one say more?

(above) **Centre Drum of George Irvin & Sons' 'Galloping Horses'.**

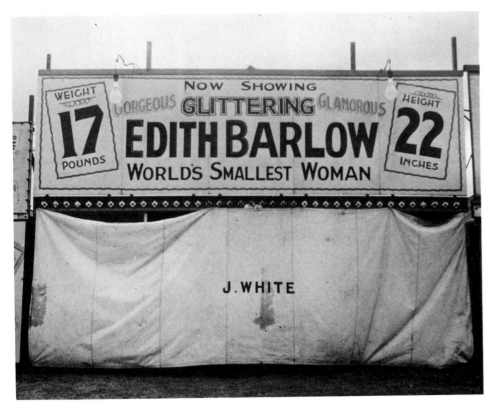

The following are short biographical notes on some of the leading personalities referred to in the text.

Allchin, William
Globe Works, Augustin Street, Northampton—steam engine builder also famous for road engines including at least one *traction* supplied to a showman. In the early 1900's Fred Gray, of London, took delivery of ' Shamrock ', No. 1246. F. W. Allchin patented a roundabout, the cars of which were constructed in the form of miniature wheels No. 9473 in 1889. The Looper (see Glossary) was based on this design.

Chapman, Nellie *(left)*
known professionally as Pauline de Vere and wife of the first Lord George Sanger. As ' Queen of the Lions ' she appeared with the Bostock and Wombwell Show. See also *Seventy Years a Showman* by Lord George Sanger.

Collins, Patrick
perhaps the most famous of all travelling showmen, a former mayor of Walsall, a J.P., and President of the Showmen's Guild from 1908 to 1928.
    Patentee of many improvements to the roundabout from a collapsible *gondola* (1894—No. 18808) to the Velocipede. His own headquarters at Bloxwich, Staffs, were known as 'Gondola Works'.
    Owner of innumerable roundabouts and traction engines, his descendants still carry on the business in various parts of the country. The Pat Collins circuit, which includes Nottingham Goose Fair, is still a good run.

Dickinson, F. W.
pioneer of electric traction, and manufacturer of dynamos. The showmen's acceptance of his proposals was delayed only by the unwieldy generating engines —horses, not steam engines, were the most common form of haulage in the 1890's—and by the extreme sensitivity of these engines to imperfect alignment.
    As early as 1892 he patented a system for electric-drive switchbacks, but it was not until 1910 that his ideas were put into practice by showmen Farrar & Tyler.

Gavioli, Ludovic
master organ builder and founder of the Societé Gavioli et Cie. See also *Mechanical Musical Instruments* by Alexander Buchner, and *A Pictorial History of the Carousel* by Frederick Fried.

Lakin, R. J.
originally joinery foreman for Orton, Sons & Spooner in Burton-upon-Trent, he later set up in business at Besley St., Streatham. Here many of the finest Arks, Waltzers, Dodg'em tracks and Swirls were produced.

The carver's skill is evident in his earlier machines, but most of his works belong to the transitional period in decoration. The robust quality of the later *varnished wrappings* era showed an equally high degree of competence.

Structural sense and an underlying architectural form were always a characteristic feature.

The business in Besley St. has been taken over by Edwin Hall, but coin-freed devices now predominate.

Marenghi, C. H.
foreman for Gavioli et Cie until a financial crisis threatened the firm. Then he left, taking with him some of the best workmen and most of the trade secrets.

At his own factory in Paris, Marenghi produced many fine organs, and in 1907 he patented a system whereby the electric lights that decorated the proscenium were made to flash in time with the music (Patent No. 217).

See also *Mechanical Musical Instruments* by Alexander Buchner.

Orton, George, Sons & Spooner
of Burton-upon-Trent—roundabout builders, famous for the superb quality of their carved work. Established at the turn of the century, they embellished many of the organs imported from Gaviolis and Marenghis to form magnificent prosceniums for 'Bioscope Shows'.

Although they did not build 'Galloping Horse' roundabouts, they did carve the *horses* and *cockerels* for many sets.

One of the first big machines was a 'Motor-Car Scenic' for Holland Brothers in 1912. Thereafter a succession of fabulous Scenics was produced, and later there were Arks and Dodg'ems.

The firm is still in existence but no longer engaged in roundabout building. Repairs and re-painting are still undertaken for special customers.

In addition to amusement devices many fine showmens' living vans were built at Burton-upon-Trent.

Savage, Frederick *(facing page)*
engineer and master roundabout builder of King's Lynn, Norfolk.

Born on 3rd March 1828 in Hevingham, Norfolk, his parents were handloom weavers. At the age of 16 he entered the employ of Thomas Cooper, Whitesmith and Machine Maker in East Dereham. In 1850 he set up his own smithy and foundry in Mermaid and Fountain Yard, Tower Street, King's Lynn.

Improved drainage in the Fens led to mechanisation in agriculture on an unprecedented scale, and, in common with other engineers in Norfolk, Savage soon became fully involved with repairs to agricultural machinery, and in building threshing machines, elevators and portable steam engines. He originated a chain-drive traction engine (with steersman in front) a single ploughing engine and tackle, and the Darby Broadside Digger (see *Savages Ltd. A Short History 1850–1964* by Ronald H. Clark).

In the late 1860's his interest extended to the machinery of the fairground, and a new era began. The Tower Street premises had long since been abandoned—so too had larger workshops off Railway Road and also in St. Nicholas Street. In 1872 he established St. Nicholas Ironworks close to the docks, and here he built Estuary House—the Savage homestead for many years and, today, occupied by the works manager.

The building of roundabouts, and the expansion and prosperity it brought, is covered more fully in the text. In the early days, the style of 'Frederick Savage—Engineer' sufficed; later, in 1893, a limited liability company was formed—'Frederick Savage & Company Ltd.' In 1898, after his death, the company was re-organised and named 'Savage Brothers Ltd.' With full order books and a further expansion programme under way, there occurred a sudden and mysterious collapse. Whether this was because of the failure of the RAC Gold Medal steam wagon or because other members of the family withdrew their capital has never been fully explained. Rumour, perhaps ill-founded, has it that one of the sons died in poverty—a match-seller on the streets of London. But a major rescue operation was launched by a local businessman—Sir Holcombe Ingleby—and the company and the livelihood of its many employees were saved. In November 1911 it received the present-day registration of 'Savages Ltd.'

Frederick Savage died on 27th April 1897. His funeral in Lynn was a memorable occasion attended by many distinguished showmen as well as civic dignitaries. All of his workmen were given black gloves—they were also given a half-crown and one day's holiday.

The illustration shows a monument erected to his honour—the only statue of its kind in King's Lynn. In addition to his distinguished career as an engineer, Frederick Savage was appointed a J.P., and was mayor in the years 1889–90.

Thurston, Henry
founder of a family of showmen who, for generations, have presented some of the finest Rides and shows ever to tour the Norwich and Eastern Counties area.

Formerly a brick-maker, it is claimed he invented the *frog,* a type of brick, and was

thereafter known as Froggy Thurston.

Continuing a fine tradition, his grandsons John, Stanley—affectionately known as Bowler Bill—and Henry J. are Riding Masters, and so too are great-grandsons Charles, Stanley Jnr., John (son of Stanley) and William.

See also 'The House of Thurston' by Tom Pearce, *East Anglian and Essex Countryside Annual*, 1965.

'The Peoples Testimonial to F. Savage, Esq.,' A permanent remembrance in Portland Stone, this statue was erected to commemorate Frederick Savage's term of office as Mayor. At the unveiling ceremony on May 27th, 1892, Lord Henry Bentinck observed 'this statue will serve to remind my constituents when they come into town on Tuesday (Market Day) that they must walk uprightly, and be kind and generous'. This observation was acclaimed with cheers.

Appendix III : BIBLIOGRAPHY

E. H. Bostock
Menageries, Circuses and Theatres.
Chapman & Hall, London, 1927.

P. W. Bradley
Some Notes on the Development of Fairground Machinery. A series of articles published in *The Engineer* in 1954, 1955 and 1957.

Alexander Buchner
Mechanical Musical Instruments.
Batchworth Press, London.

Ronald H. Clark, A.M.I.Mech.E.
Savages Limited, Engineers, St. Nicholas Ironworks, King's Lynn—A Short History 1850–1964. Modern Press, Norwich.
Chronicles of a Country Works.
Percival Marshall, London, 1952.

Antony Hippisley Coxe
A Seat at the Circus. Evans Brothers, London, 1951.

T. F. G. Dexter
The Pagan Origin of Fairs. New Knowledge Press, Perranporth, 1930.

M. Willson Disher
Fairs, Circuses and Music Halls.
William Collins, London, 1941.

Arthur Fay
Bioscope Shows and Their Engines.
Oakwood Press, Lingfield Surrey, 1966.

Frederick Fried
A Pictorial History of The Carousel.
A. S. Barnes & Co. Inc., New York, 1964.

T. Frost
The Old Showmen and the Old London Fairs. 1874.

Barbara Jones
The Unsophisticated Arts. Architectural Press, London, 1951.

Samuel McKechnie
Popular Entertainment through the Ages.
Sampson Low, London, 1931.

Henry Morley
Memoirs of Bartholomew Fair.
Chapman and Hall, London, 1859.
Memoirs of Bartholomew Fair.
Geo. Routledge & Sons, Glasgow, 1892.

R. W. Muncey
Our Old English Fairs. The Sheldon Press, London, 1936.

Peter Mundy
The Travels of Peter Mundy in Europe and Asia, 1608–1667. Hakluyt Society, London Vol. 1, 1907–36.

Thomas Murphy, M.B.E.
The Evolution of Amusement Machines. A Paper presented at the Royal Society of Arts and subsequently printed in their journal, London, 7th September 1951.

W. Owen
The Book of Fairs published by the King's Authority. London, 1759.

Tom Pearce
The House of Thurston. Article in *East Anglian and Essex Countryside Annual*, 1965.

L. T. C. Rolt
The Swan Song of Steam. Article in The Saturday Book, No. 15, edited by John Hadfield.

F. C. Roope, M.A.
Come to the Fair. The World's Fair. Oldham, Lancs.

'Lord' George Sanger
Seventy Years a Showman. Dent. London, 1926.

Sir Garrard Tyrwhitt-Drake
The English Circus and Fairground. Methuen, London, 1946.

C. Walford
Fairs, Past and Present. Elliot Stock, London, 1883.

In addition to the foregoing *The Worlds Fair*, a weekly journal published in Oldham, is essentially the showmen's paper and, to the patient and discerning reader, a mine of information.

The following Collections are unique, and offer scope for further study:—

> Fenwick Collection, Laing Art Gallery, Newcastle-upon-Tyne.
> Thomas Walker Collection, Tewkesbury Museum, Tewkesbury.

There are some documents of interest at the King's Lynn Museum and at the Guildhall Museum London.

Among many fine collections of fairground organs are those of Mr. W. J. Barlow at Cleobury Mortimer, Mr. George Cushing of Laurel Farm, Thursford, and Mr. Tom Alberts of Bolton, Lancs.

Societies for the enthusiast include the Fairground Society, British Fairground Society, Fair Organ Preservation Society and the Friendship Circle of Showland Fans.

Appendix IV: A CALENDAR OF FAIRS

The unqualified number and diversity of events held during the year makes the preparation of a complete list an impossible task. Also the fluctuation in Saints' Days, festivals and so on, not least the incidence of Easter Day, produces an infinitely variable pattern of events. From time to time locations alter, and in isolated cases, cancellations occur because of water logged ground or the indisposition or death of a showman.

The selection here presented is a random one, but some of the more interesting events are included. Many of these are held under royal charter and their perpetuity is more or less assured. An attempt has been made to represent all parts of the British Isles. The town hall or police station is the best place to confirm the venue and the exact opening days.

February

King's Lynn Mart

The first event of the season, this ancient fair opens on St. Valentine's Day. The charter was granted by Henry VIII in 1537. The Tuesday Market Place, where the amusements assemble, is first blessed by the Chaplain. An elaborate opening ceremony is performed by the Mayor, Aldermen and Councillors.

March

Grantham Mid Lent Fair
Stamford (Lincs.) Fair

Easter

Bank Holidays are celebrated in most cities with a fair of 3 or 4 days duration—in some cases a full week. Among the most famous are those held on London's Heaths and Commons.

Blackheath, London

Hampton Court Green, Middlesex.

Hampstead Heath, London.

Richmond Old Deer Park, Surrey.

Wanstead Flats, London.

Huddersfield, Yorks.

Ipswich, Suffolk.

Norwich, Norfolk.

Tunbridge Wells, Kent.

April

Derby Charter Fair

generally the week following Easter.

Kirkcaldy Links Market

a spectacular street fair occupying $1\frac{1}{2}$ miles of the Esplanade, and reputed to be the largest in the world. In recent years there have been as many as 40 rides, 2 circuses and 10 large shows.

May

Boston May Fair

Opens the first Wednesday or Thursday.

Hereford May Fair
the first Wednesday and for 2 following days.

Princes Risborough May Fair
the first Thursday and for 2 following days.

Beaconsfield, Bucks
a one-day street fair generally held on the 10th.

Epsom Derby Fair
for 7 days.

Whitsun
Acton Carnival, London.
Blackheath, London.
Hampstead Heath, London.
Richmond Old Deer Park, Surrey.
Coventry, Warwicks.
Northampton.

June
Pinner (Middlesex) Street Fair
generally held on the 9th.

Newcastle Town Moor Festival
known locally as the 'Hoppings', one of the largest fairs of the season. The layout, with rides arranged in a *grand avenue* and flanked on both sides by *joints* and booths, is unique.

Cambridge Midsummer Fair
a gigantic triangle of amusements, the river on one side and a tumble of living vans and packing trunks in the middle. There are still china and linoleum stalls but it is a tenuous link with the great fair established by King John in 1211.

July
Glasgow Green Fair
Durham Miners' Gala

Aikey Brae Fair, Aberdeenshire
a unique fair of ancient origin held on the last Sunday in July, and only in recent years on the Friday and Saturday before. The *gaff* is in the hills some 20 miles north of Aberdeen.

August
Lindfield Village Common Fair
generally opens on the 8th and for 2 following days.

Mitcham Fair
one of the largest fairs in the London area, the opening ceremony is symbolised with a golden key.

September
Oxford St. Giles Fair
Monday and Tuesday following the first Sunday.

Neath Pleasure Fair
Barnstaple Mop Fair
Gloucester Barton Fair

Barnet (Herts.) Horse Fair
formerly an important cattle fair—now predominantly a pleasure fair, although there is still some dealing in horses and ponies.

St. Matthew's Fair, Bridgewater, Somerset
last Wednesday.

Newbury (Berks.) Michaelmas Fair

October
Abingdon (Berks.) Michaelmas Fair
first Monday.

Peterborough Bridge Fair
first week.

Nottingham Goose Fair
first Thursday and 2 following days—many famous showland families combine on this 11 acre *gaff*.

Hull Pleasure Fair
generally opens on the 11th for 7 days—the original charter was granted by Edward I in 1299. The amusements fill a 14 acre site which is approached by a half mile street of stalls.

King's Norton Mop Fair
Monday nearest the 12th.

Stratford-upon-Avon Mop Fair
generally the 12th—the first of two Mops, and the larger.

St. Ives (Hunts.) Fair
Witney Big Mop Fair
Banbury Michaelmas Fair
Chichester Sloe Fair
Birmingham Onion Fair
Haverfordwest Charter Fair

November
Poole Fair
first week.

Pembroke Winter Fair

Loughborough
virtually the last event of the season.

December
Norwich Christmas Fair
the many families who winter in or around Norwich assemble for this chilly spectacle.

The Illustrations

Every care has been taken to ensure proper acknowledgement to the copyright holders but in many cases, the material has been handed on second and third hand. As a result the true origin becomes obscure.

Index